TERRORISM IN THE 1980s

EDGAR O'BALLANCE

ARMS AND
ARMOUR

First published in Great Britain in 1989 by Arms and Armour Press, Artillery House, Artillery Row, London SW1P 1RT

Distributed in the USA by Sterling Publishing Co. Inc., 2 Park Avenue, New York, NY 10016

Distributed in Australia by Capricorn Link (Australia) Pty. Ltd., P.O. Box 665, Lane Cove, New South Wales 2066, Australia

British Library Cataloguing in Publication Data:
O'Ballance, Edgar
1. Terrorism
322.4'2
ISBN 0-85368-925-3

Designed and edited by DAG Publications Ltd. Designed by David Gibbons; edited by Michael Boxall; typeset by Ronset Typesetters, Darwen; printed and bound in Great Britain by Mackays of Chatham, PLC, Letchworth, Herts.

GLOSSARY

ASU	Active Service Unit (IRA)	IRP	Islamic Republican Party
BKA	Federal Criminal Office (West Germany)	KWP	Kurdish Workers' Party
		Majlis	Iranian Parliament
CIA	Central Intelligence Agency (USA)	MNF	Multi-National Force (Lebanon)
CRS	French Para-military Police		
DGSE	French Overseas Intelligence Agency	*Mossad*	Israeli Secret Service
		NATO	North Atlantic Treaty Organization
DST	French Internal Intelligence Agency		
DUP	Democratic Unionist Party (Northern Ireland)	NI	Northern Ireland
		NORAID	Northern Aid (IRA front in the USA)
EEC	European Economic Community		
		Pentiti	Italian Supergrass System
Ertzantza	Basque Regional Police	PNV	Basque Nationalist Party
Euskadiko Eskerra	ETA-PM's political wing	RC	Roman Catholic
		ROI	Republic of Ireland
Fianna Fail	Irish Political Party	RTE	Irish Radio and Television
		RUC	Royal Ulster Constabulary
Gardai Siochana	Irish Police Force	SAS	Special Air Service (Britain)
		SCIRI	Supreme Council of the Islamic Revolution for Iraq
GIGN	French Anti-Terrorist Force		
GN	French Police	SDLP	Social Democratic and Labour Party (Northern Ireland)
GRT	Belgian Anti-Terrorist Police		
Herri Batasuna	ETA-M's political wing		
		SLA	South Lebanon Army
Huntchak	Armenian Political Party	SSNP	Syrian Socialist Nationalist Party
ICO	Islamic Conference Organization	TCP	Turkish Communist Party
		UATC	Unified Anti-Terrorist Command (Spain)
Ikorpina	Basque flag		
IRC	International Red Cross	UDR	Ulster Defence Regiment (Britain)
IRNA	Islamic Republic News Agency		

CONTENTS

GLOSSARY OF TERRORIST ORGANIZATIONS

Anti-Communist Alliance (Spanish anti-ETA)

AD — Direct Action (French)

al-Jihad al-Islami — Islamic Holy War (Lebanon)

Amal — Hope (Lebanese Shiite Militia)

April 7 Group — (Italy)

ARM — Armenian Revolutionary Movement

ARO — Armed Revolutionary Organization (Portugal)

ASALA — Armenian Secret Army for the Liberation of Armenia

Bewegung 2 Juni — Second June Movement (West Berlin)

Black Order — (Italy)

BVE — Spanish Basque Battalion (anti-ETA group)

CAA — Anti-Capitalist Autonomous Command (Spanish)

CCC — Fighting Communist Cells (Belgian)

CSPPA — Committee for Solidarity with Middle Eastern and Arab Political Prisoners

Dashnag-Sution — Armenian Revolutionary Federation

DFLA — Democratic Front for the Liberation of Armenia

EE — Basque Left

EOKA — National Organization of the Cypriot Struggle for Unity with Greece

ETA — Basque Homeland and Liberty

ETA-M — ETA-Militar

ETA-PM — ETA-Politico-Militar

FARC — Armed Revolutionary Forces of Colombia

FARL — Lebanese Armed Revolutionary Faction

Fatah — Victory (Palestinian mainstream group of Arafat)

Fatah-RC — Fatah-Revolutionary Council

FLB-AR — Breton Liberation Front-Republican Army

FLN — National Liberation Front

FLNC — Corsican National Liberation Front

FLNKS — Kanak Socialist National Liberation Front

FLOSY — Front for the Liberation of South Yemen

FMLF — Farabundo Marti Liberation Front

FP-25 — Popular Forces-25th April (Portuguese)

FRELIMO — Front for the Liberation of Mozambique

FRETILIN — Revolutionary Front for the Liberation of East Timor

FUP — Popular United Forces (Portuguese)

GAE — Armed Spanish Group (anti-ETA)

GAL — Anti-Terrorist Liberation Group (Spanish anti-ETA)

GRAPO — 1st October Anti-Fascist Group (Spanish)

HB — People's Unity (Basque Political Party)

Hezbollah — Party of God (Lebanese and Iranian)

Hizb al-Daawa al Islami — Iraqi terrorist organization (Shiites)

INLA — Irish National Liberation Army

Iparretarrak — French Basque Liberation Movement

IRA — Irish Republican Army

IRSP — Irish Republican Socialist Party

JCAG — Justice Commandos of the Armenian Genocide

KAS — Basque Socialist Support Group

Kassimis — (Greece)

M-19 — 19th April Movement (Colombian)

MNLF — Moro National Liberation Front (Philippines)

MPLA — Popular Movement for the Liberation of Angola

NAP — Armed Proletarian Nucleus (Italian)

NARM — New Armenian Resistance Movement

New Order — (Italy)

November 17 Group — (Greece)

NPA — New People's Army (Philippines)

NTF — Northern Terror Front (Holland)

PLF — Palestine Liberation Front

PFLP — Popular Front for the Liberation of Palestine

PFLP-GC — PFLP-General Command

PLO — Palestine Liberation Organization

Prima Linea — Front Line (Italy)

RAF — Red Army Faction (West Germany)

RB — Red Brigades (Italian)

Revolutionary Group of International Solidarity: Cristos — (Greece)

RZ — Revolutionary Cells (West Germany)

Sinn Fein — (Ourselves Alone) Political wing of the IRA

UDA — Ulster Defence Association

UFF — Ulster Freedom Fighters

UNITA — Union of the Total Independence of Angola

UVF — Ulster Volunteer Force

Preface

INTERNATIONAL terrorism, as we think of it today, began in the late 1960s with dramatic exploits of skyjacking and hostage seizures on a grand scale. Its volume and ferocity rose to a crescendo in the 1970s, but was beginning to decline by 1980, as governments and their security forces, initially unprepared for such a form of warfare, started to get the measure of this massive new problem. Some governments even flattered themselves that they were containing, or even defeating, terrorism through improved awareness and counter-terrorist measures. But from the mid-1980s, terrorist incidents began to increase again.

As long as political repression, social injustice and extremes of wealth and poverty exist, there will be revolutionaries and political activists eager and able to rush forward to exploit such situations with the weapon of terrorism. The war against terrorism is an on-going one that may never end. Governments and terrorists will each have successes and failures. Few terrorist groups achieve their political aim, but they do cause governments embarrassment, harassment, and sometimes force them to yield to blackmail. Generally, terrorists have far more failures than successes, and their exploits are simply tactical victories, not strategic ones, as governments seldom fall to terrorist pressure.

Five terrorist organizations have been chosen for this brief study because they reflect the current terrorist spectrum. They differ in their aims, motivations, and tactics; and the various security forces have responded with a range of measures to counter the threat they pose. Euro-Terrorism International, consisting of extremist left-wing groups, dedicated to disrupting NATO and bringing down certain Western governments, peaked in the mid-1980s, but since then has declined. The Hezbollah is a combination of state terrorism and Shia Muslim Fundamentalism prepared to operate suicide missions. The IRA and ETA have 'nationalist' aims, both struggling to achieve their own form of national independence; while the Armenian groups are fighting for a 'homeland' in Turkey, a seemingly forlorn hope.

The spelling of names, especially foreign ones, sometimes tends to be a problem as there are alternatives to chose from; when this is so, the one chosen is that accepted by general consensus. For brevity, sets of initials are frequently used to represent designations, and any seeming discrepancy between initials and designations is accounted for by the English translation being used.

Edgar O'Ballance

1. The Nature of Terrorism

A Lebanese Shiite fighter symbolizes the faceless terror that stalks the Middle East; face masked to conceal his identity and to increase the menacing effect, the militiaman brandishes a folding-stock AK-47 while guarding a barricade in the southern suburbs of Beirut. (Popperfoto)

'Terror is an absolute necessity in time of revolution'

– Dzerzhinsky (Stalin's Chief of Police)

TERRORISM is a weapon that can be desperately dangerous, or counter-productive, and like other weapons, such as the sword and the gun, its effectiveness depends on how skilfully it is wielded. The stock-in-trade of terrorism is to arouse the human emotion of fear, thus intimidating a person to do, or not to do, something against his will. The multiplicity of human fears range from vague uneasiness to an acute state of anxiety, and from mild apprehension to abject terror. Different people have different fears, and one person's fear is often another's thrill. Some suffer from vertigo, while others enjoy parachuting; some suffer from claustrophobia, while others enjoy pot-holing; and men are generally indifferent to spiders, which usually horrify women. Most people fear death, or at least the manner of dying, and all fear pain, injury, torture or mutilation. These familiar everyday fears are the butt for the weapon of terrorism.

The weapon of terrorism includes torture, that most feared of human activities, and once common to extract information from unwilling lips. It is used as a punishment, in vengeance, for retribution and occasionally through sheer sadism. It is doubtful whether torture has ever ceased to exist: it has always lurked in dark corners of the earth, being far more prevalent than supposed, or even imagined. To mention a single example, in 1979, Salim-el-Lozi, an outspoken editor working in England, returned to his native Lebanon to attend his mother's funeral. He was kidnapped, and his tortured body was later found. While he was still alive, his hands had been dipped into acid to strip off all the flesh, to be left resting on a typewriter. His fate was intended to discourage others from writing in a similar vein.

In the 1980s, many tortured bodies have been found in Northern Ireland, western Europe, the Middle East and elsewhere in the world. Torture and death seem almost as widespread today as they ever were in the so-called barbaric ages. Amnesty International records such incidents in their thousands. Modern implements of torture have simply changed from the rack, wheel and thumb-screw to electrodes, the electric drill and the chain-saw. Knee-capping, laming and dropping blocks of concrete on hands and feet as punishment continue to produce living examples of terrorism.

The Roots of Terrorism

The objective of political terrorism is to force a government, a people or a group of people to surrender to political blackmail or subjugation. (Terrorism for purely criminal purposes is not considered in this study.) The spark that often ignites insurrection, with attendant use of the weapon of terrorism, is sustained exploitation and repression of a people; they become politically frustrated and seething with discontent, ready to be roused into desperate action by crusading revolutionary leaders such as Mao Tse-tung, Ho Chi Minh, Abdul Gamal Nasser and Yasser Arafat. These men, inspired by the writings of Marx, Lenin, Trotsky and other agitating prophets, are the exponents of revolution and violence; but since revolutions can be crushed by military force, the weak have to find another way. Those prepared to use illegal force resort to the weapon of terrorism, whereby small numbers can create a climate of apprehension and fear. The excessive emphasis on majority rule in the liberal democracies can cause similar frustration – the ballot box can seem of little use to repressed minority groups with grievances. This dictatorship of the majority, and a reluctance to change, are the basis for the on-going insurgencies in both Northern Ireland and the Philippines.

With its political motivation, careful planning, and shrewd direction, the weapon of terrorism has frequently been referred to as the 'poor man's warfare'. Modern technology enables tiny groups, or even one person, to wield gigantic power of death and destruction out of all proportion to conventional numbers and the resources of governments. Its cost is minuscule compared with the smallest conventional military campaign or operation, or even a single sophisticated weapon-system, such as a modern combat aircraft or a nuclear warhead. This was cruelly evident in June 1985, when a Sikh Separatist allegedly placed a small explosive charge aboard an Air India Boeing 747 airliner, causing it to crash in the Atlantic Ocean, just off Ireland, with the loss of the aircraft and all 329 people aboard.

Acts of violence or intimidation against established authority are generally considered to be 'terrorism' in the modern sense of that expression, if the declared or implied motive is political, even though the acts themselves may be strictly criminal, such as shooting, causing an explosion or operating a 'protection racket'. Groups and individuals using terrorism loudly emphasize their political motives as justifications, rejecting any criminal connotation to their activities.

Those who resort to using the weapon of terrorism often consider themselves to be 'freedom fighters' struggling against oppression to establish a legitimate and desirable political objective. This is particularly so in Third World countries where the conflict is against colonial masters or dictators. On the other hand, established authorities consider them to be 'insurgent terrorists' with subversive intentions. Hence, the well-worn expression, 'One man's terrorist is another man's freedom fighter'.

The Classifications of Terror

In the popular mind, all who use the weapon of terrorism are 'terrorists'. But while there can be little argument on the definition of terrorism, there may be less agreement as to who precisely is a 'terrorist' and what is a 'terrorist organization', since the weapon of terrorism is used by many, some for only a short while or to a particular end. For the purpose of this study terrorists can be divided broadly into three categories: rural terrorists, urban terrorists, and international terrorists. No one knows exactly how many terrorists there are in the world at any one time, except that rural terrorists, such as those who serve in guerrilla-type insurgent armies, must number in the hundred thousands, while urban terrorists probably only number in their thousands, and international ones in their hundreds.

Rural examples are the New People's Army (NPA) in the Philippines which is over 20,000 strong; the Farabundo Marti Liberation Front of El Salvador almost 10,000 strong; and the Tamil insurgents in Sri Lanka which were once more than 13,000 strong.

These are guerrilla-type resistance armies, usually in under-developed countries, using the weapon of terror against established authority as a necessary stage of their revolution. To group them together with the much smaller number of urban terrorists and the relatively tiny numbers of sophisticated international terrorists gives only a crude general picture, but it boosts figures for the vested interests of various national intelligence agencies.

The Rural Path   Political power in the modern world lies in population centres, and when insurgents are driven from cities or are unable to obtain a firm hold in them, they are forced, often unwillingly, to take the rural path to revolution. The most notable example of this was that of the Chinese Communist leader, Mao Tse-tung, a political crusading missionary if there ever was one, whose tiny Red Army was driven from the cities by the Nationalists and forced into the 'Long March' (retreat) to a remote area simply in order to survive. There Mao rethought his strategy and a 'guerrilla army' was formed. It was expanded and conditioned before eventually returning to the offensive and forcing Nationalist armies southwards and its leaders eventually into flight to Taiwan.

The so-called Mao Tse-tung 'blue-print' for successful revolutionary war has been the inspiration of many a revolutionary visionary or practitioner ever since. The genesis in Mao's case was the coming together of a group of like-minded, dedicated revolutionaries with a political message and ambition, who issued a manifesto, and then struggled for survival and recognition. Terror was used as 'a necessary instrument' to force an alien doctrine on peasants to become 'the sea in which the guerrilla fish could swim'. The methods consisted of assassination or intimidation of local officials and those reluctant to convert. And, since the ambition of rural peasants everywhere is to own the plot of land they work, rather than merely to exchange masters, 'land reform' became a central promise of the revolutionaries.

The next stage was to form and arm small groups to operate the pin-pricking tactics of avoidance to over-stretch and demoralize government troops – in other words operate 'guerrilla warfare – and then to move on to a trial of strength, known as the 'protracted warfare' stage, to sap government will and resources. 'Mobile warfare', a form of conventional warfare, followed, during which the Chinese Red Armies used the weapon of terror, as would any army not bound by the Geneva Conventions.

The Mao Tse-tung blue print was successful in Indo-China in 1954, in Vietnam in 1975, and in Nicaragua in 1979; but it has also failed, especially in South America, where his disciple Che Guevara, was killed by Security Forces in Bolivia in 1966. Successes have been in countries where expanses of mountains, forests and jungles afford full rein to guerrilla mobility; all used the weapon of terror in the early stages, but it was only one factor in the ultimate victory. Opposing governments countered with the same weapon, which generally played into the hands of the insurgents by alienating the people from the government.

The Urban Path Revolutionary organizations anxious to snatch political power from sitting governments usually favour a base in the big cities, where the squalor of shanty town life offers a teeming mass of potential revolutionaries: thousands of landless peasants, unemployed, the deprived, discontented and hungry. The activists play upon discontent, coupling it with a political message that hits against government policies, agitating, converting and recruiting. The weapon of terror is used to eliminate, or intimidate, policemen, government officials and informers, to bring sections of the community to heel, so the revolutionaries can shelter within them. It is naturally much the same in the Western world owing to its heavy urbanization, with would-be revolutionaries basing themselves on major cities if they can, where they are more anonymous. Examples are the Red Brigades in Italy, the First October Anti-Fascist Group (GRAPO) in Spain, and Action Directe in France. Because of their environment, urban terrorists tend to have a higher degree of education and sophistication than their rural guerrilla counterparts. Generally, urban terrorists tend to operate within their own localities, although they seek all the help they can get from abroad.

Dual Paths Some revolutionary organizations are able to follow a two-pronged policy of both urban and rural activity. Initially rurally based, the New People's Army in the Philippines, has reached the 'protracted stage' of guerrilla warfare in parts of the countryside. It has also recently moved into Manila (the capital) and Mindanao (the second largest city), using 'Sparrow Squads' – small assassination teams, so called because they flit quickly from place to place like sparrows, to kill policemen and soldiers, to break down law and order, and to demoralize the security forces. The toll in Manila alone in 1987 was 67. In the Punjab, in India, where Sikhs form 60 per cent of the population, Sikh militant separatists fighting for an independent state of Khalistan, are using both rural and urban tactics. Activists are sheltered in both cities and the countryside, while the weapon of terror is being used to drive the non-Sikh minority from their homes.

International Terrorism International terrorists can be said to be those who operate in one or more countries other than their own, either as activists, couriers or in a liaison capacity. Accordingly, they are more flexible, mobile and worldly-wise. International terrorist groups include the Armenian Secret Army for the Liberation of Armenia (ASALA), the Lebanese Armed Revolutionary Faction (FARL) and the Palestinian groups; these all strike at hostile targets in foreign countries, such as embassies, aircraft, airline offices, government installations and individuals, and they also indulge in hostage taking. Some urban groups, such as the Irish Republican Army (IRA), the West German Red Army Faction (RAF) and the French Action Directe, maintain a small 'international cell' for overseas contacts, but this does not change the basic character of the urban organization. For example, the ETA and the IRA have some contacts, and an ETA member regularly addresses the IRA annual convention in Dublin.

Over the years, certain countries such as Libya, Syria and South Yemen have allowed terrorists of many nationalities to attend their training camps, and this has caused fraternal links to develop between many of these groups, leading to liaison, shared intelligence, mutual assistance and sometimes active participation in joint terrorist exploits. These are the real 'international terrorists'. Palestinian terrorist groups, perhaps the originators of international terrorism as we know it today, and indeed all Middle Eastern terrorist groups, seem to have wide international contacts and operate accordingly. One set of US figures claims that 'international terrorism has touched 91 countries'; this is perhaps an exaggeration, but secret terrorist contacts do exist, although they seem to depend upon personalities getting on well together.

Nationalism Groups with political missionary roles, such as the Marxist Armed Revolutionary Forces of Colombia (FARC), despite liberal use of the weapon of terror, have difficulty in enforcing their political creed on the peasant masses. Those who raise the rallying cry of 'nationalism' have comparatively little difficulty in gaining allegiance when the call is for 'Freedom' from an alien government, and they become 'freedom fighters'. The motivation of nationalism is the most inspiring and durable. The IRA and ETA have proved to be two of the most durable of the movements that demand 'freedom', despite many set-backs and difficulties.

Current examples include the Corsican National Liberation Front (FLNC); the Kanak Socialist National Liberation Front (FLNKS) in New Caledonia; the Free Papua Movement struggling for an independent Irian Jaya; and the Marxist Revolutionary Front for the Liberation of East Timor (FRETILIN) fighting against Indonesian annexation. The motivation of nationalism has inspired groups struggling to return to their 'homeland': the Palestinian groups, and Armenian ones too calling for the return of their former 'homeland' in Turkey, fall into this category.

The Characteristics of Terrorist Groups

Leaving aside the numerous terrorists in revolutionary guerrilla armies, most urban and international terrorist groups are small, some quite tiny. Groups constantly appear, struggle for survival and recognition, merge with one another, destroy one another, are swallowed up by larger ones, and often splinter as a result of internal feuds, many eventually to become dormant, dissolve or disappear from the terrorist scene completely – like shooting-stars in the sky – most having left a barely visible trail. Few survive.

There does not seem to be a universal, comprehensive list of terrorist groups. Compiling such records obviously presents problems in obtaining accurate information because groups are secretive for reasons of survival. Intelligence agencies and national police forces are reluctant to divulge information or share it with each other, perhaps sometimes being ashamed of their own ignorance; while terrorist groups often use code-names for certain exploits in order to confuse the authorities. Countries also vary in their definitions of terrorism; many simply 'do not want to know' or become involved in such documentation.

The US State Department periodically issues sets of figures on terrorism, but these tend to be suspect – they over-inflate for vested-interest motives. However, these figures are occasionally quoted as there are few other reliable terrorist statistics openly available of any value. One set of US figures opines that there may be a thousand terrorist organizations in the world, and perhaps ten thousand active terrorists – which must mean the groups only average about ten members – and obviously the larger guerrilla armies are not included. Perhaps the best 'guesstimate' is that there may be a hundred or more urban and international groups, of which perhaps thirty or so have become household names, having gained and held media attention by their dramatic exploits or their flair for publicity.

Strata Most urban and international groups seem to be of somewhat similar composition, being headed by a small echelon of 'top terrorists'. These leaders and activists, sometimes less than a dozen, are often clustered around a dominant individual, and these are the names that become known to the public. They are supported by larger numbers of lesser-calibre adherents who can perform such essential tasks as gathering intelligence, guarding the leadership, arms caches and hostages, providing safe-houses, procuring materials, and acting as messengers and look-outs. Some are used for minor exploits. The US State Department has estimated that about 80 per cent of all terrorist acts recorded consist of planting explosives with timing detonators, throwing grenades, positioning car-bombs or shooting victims in ambush, all of which give the terrorist a good survival margin and still make a big impact on victims and bystanders.

Recruitment A fascinating question, often asked, is: how does one become a terrorist? The general answer is that an individual is attracted to a certain cause and seeks to join it; or a terrorist organization seeks out an individual as being suitable to further its cause. Some, living in 'repressed' communities, are conditioned from birth by their elders and become willing recruits when they become old enough, as in the Basque territory of Spain, in Corsica and in the Nationalist areas of Northern Ireland, where 'alien' governments and their symbols of authority are the hated 'enemy'; and in Palestinian, and other, refugee camps. With 'nationalism' as the rallying cry, there is seldom any dearth of recruits, but terrorist groups with a political message to put across find difficulties and often search for suitable candidates on university campuses – it is often said that to become a successful 'top terrorist' a university degree is almost mandatory.

The first demands on a recruit are dedication and loyalty. In urban groups this is of much greater importance than in revolutionary guerrilla armies, which can develop the military *esprit de corps* and enforce military discipline. The recruit must first of all accept the group's political cause: he must become wholeheartedly dedicated to that cause and be prepared to devote his life and energy to furthering it. He thus mounts a tiger and cannot dismount, for he knows too much about his group. If he deserts and is caught, he will be executed, and probably tortured first.

If not already dedicated and conditioned by childhood environment and background, continuous indoctrination will keep ideals brightly burnished. If anyone doubts the effectiveness of indoctrination, consider the case of Patricia Hearst, who was kidnapped in the United States, by the tiny Simbionese Liberation Army, a group with vaguely nihilist aims. Ten weeks after her capture she was helping the SLA rob a bank apparently quite willingly. Under pressure, terrorists quite often have to scatter and go to ground, or are ordered to become 'sleepers' until required to become active again. Many are 'lost', being already out of circulation when their group disintegrates.

The effectiveness of any organization that uses the weapon of terrorism, depends upon the calibre of the leadership and activists. Leaders, especially founder-members, are not usually extrovert characters with a bombastic manner, but rather the opposite, careful in speech and action, with the quiet conviction that they have found the only true path towards their ultimate aim. Most leaders and activists are completely dedicated to their cause, although there are still a few to whom the term 'psychopath' may well apply, who are there for the violence rather than the cause. But there can even be a role for them. Dessie O'Hare, the so-called 'Border Fox', was more a bandit and pyschopath than a dedicated revolutionary, reputedly having been a member of both the Provisional IRA and the Irish National Liberation Army (INLA). He led the Irish *Gardai* (Police) a spectacular chase, continually escaping, until finally cornered, wounded and captured in a shoot-out in November 1987. He was charged with 27 murders and was reputed to have committed more. There are exceptions. Carlos, 'The Jackal', who gained terrorist notoriety in the 1970s, was a terrorist leader by vocation rather than by simple dedication, the cause being of lesser importance. This could be said of other terrorist leaders today, such as Abu Nidal (of Fatah-Revolutionary Council), Georges Ibrahim Abdullah (of FARL), and Jean-Marc Rouillon (of Action Directe).

Terrorist leaders and activists must have the 'killer instinct' and be able to kill to order a certain person at a certain place at a certain time – many people can kill in anger, passion, or in the heat of battle as trained soldiers, but few can kill in cold blood. They must also be devoid of all pity and remorse, which so few of us are, since their victims may include women and children; they may have to throw a grenade into a café or place a bomb on an aircraft, when the result would be indiscriminate death and mutilation. Those who undertake suicide missions do not come into this category, for they are not required to think or reason. Their indoctrination is exceptional and hinges upon their having certain religious beliefs, which are played upon by their masters. Generally, successful terrorist groups hold no brief for the old-time 'mindless' thug or gunman.

Indeed, terrorist leaders and activists require a fairly high standard of intelligence, education, sophistication and technical knowledge, as they have to initiate, plan and carry through complicated operations. Consider all the detail that must be examined to organize just a simple skyjack exploit. Information has to be obtained, sifted and assessed. As the terrorists must work together as a team, a high degree of reliability, steadiness and self-discipline is also needed. They must be able to keep one jump ahead of the security forces; should be fluent in English, the international language, if it is not their native one, and perhaps have the mastery of another major language if they operate in a particular country; should be able to travel without seeming out of place or inviting suspicion; have a knowledge of foreign customs and be familiar with air travel conditions; should understand firearms and explosives; and be familiar with all modern means of communication.

Obviously, a high degree of courage is necessary. To carry out terrorist exploits, they risk death, serious injury, capture, long imprisonment and in some countries torture as well. Such daring was exercised in November 1987, when a 20-year-old member of the Popular Front for the Liberation of Palestine-General Command (PFLP-GC), flew a motorized hang-glider from Syria over the border into northern Israel. On landing he killed six Israeli soldiers and wounded seven more before being killed himself.

A terrorist does not have to be a man – there are many women terrorists, some of whom are efficient and deadly. For example, 12 of the 22 founder-members of the Baader-Meinhof Gang were women, as were 30 per cent of the Japanese Red Army, while at least two of the four-person leadership of Action Directe were also women. The alleged leader of the Provisional IRA Active Service Unit (ASU) planning to commit a spectacular explosion in Gibraltar in March 1988, was Mairead Farrell, who, with her two companions, was shot dead by the British Special Air Service Regiment (SAS). In Lebanon in the 1980s several girls and young women, singled out by the Hezbollah, have carried out suicide missions.

A question often asked, prompted no doubt by dramatic fiction, is whether a sinister terrorist 'master-mind' lurks in the background like a spider in its web? Certainly, Wadieh Hadad, a Palestinian, who probably organized most of the major international terrorist exploits from 1968 until his death in 1978, could have been regarded as such a character; but although by 1980, there was at times a considerable amount of international terrorist liaison and co-operation, and certain prominent terrorist leaders were becoming widely known for their many exploits, none seemed to fit exactly into such a role.

Finance Apart from having a political cause and a degree of popular support, willing or forced, to operate successfully urban terrorist groups need certain assets, the two most important being money and publicity. There are others, of course, that govern their effectiveness and even survival, but they usually have a lesser priority. With money, terrorists can buy practically all the material things needed, such as weapons, explosives, information, safe-houses, food, travel – and a person's silence. You name it and invariably it can be bought if sufficient money, blended perhaps with a touch of fear, is available. Terrorists believe that every material object has its monetary value, and every individual has his price.

Money is generally obtained by three methods, all criminal in themselves: kidnapping for ransom, various forms of theft, and protection rackets. Terrorists regard themselves as being at war. When criticized for using such criminal means, they point out the devious and doubtful practices employed by nations when at war with one another. Bank robberies are common, but steady incomes are derived from protection rackets on businesses and individuals. The Palestinian El Fatah group has persuaded certain Arab governments that employ Palestinian workers to deduct 5 per cent from their wages and hand it over to the Palestine Liberation Organization (PLO) – like a sort of terrorist tax levy. Both the PLO and IRA groups raise money from their expatriates, using more than a little intimidation.

A few terrorist groups, like El Fatah, have become wealthy in their own right, having shrewdly invested money and purchased property and business concerns in several countries. Others are less prudent, or less fortunate, and scrape along in conjunction with criminal elements, as happens often in Italy. Seizing hostages for ransom money instead of for political purposes helps some groups survive financially. Active terrorist groups always seem to be able to obtain money; others, lacking sufficient determination and capability, have difficulty in surviving.

Recently it has become obvious that certain urban and international terrorist groups have become involved in, or had contacts with, the lucrative drug-trafficking business, especially those with roots in the Middle East or South America. The once sparsely cultivated Beka'a Valley in Lebanon is now covered in the season with a multiplicity of swathes of 'green' fields of hashish-producing hemp.

Publicity It has often been said that the media need the terrorists as much as the terrorists need the media. Terrorists certainly need publicity. If their deeds are unknown and unrecorded, their effectiveness decreases: no one knows anything about them or their causes, and neither do they care. The terrorists must demonstrate to the world at large their destructive powers and their will to use them. Terrorists need the media to help them generate fear, and the more spectacular the exploit the more publicity is obtained. This tends to cause a 'one-upmanship' rivalry between major terrorist groups. Terrorists hunger for attention, especially the smaller groups, and this leads many to make false claims of responsibility for exploits in order to get themselves noticed.

In Western democracies the free media help terrorists spread their reputation of terror freely and widely, which is of immense advantage to them. Many other countries have some form of censorship, which can be manipulated to the terrorists' disadvantage. Rigid censorship, for example, explains why we know so little about terrorism and terrorists in the Soviet Union and have to rely upon scraps of information of bombing incidents in Georgia and rumours of explosions in some of the Central Asian Muslim republics.

Terrorism has ironically been described as 'theatre', with terrorists, security forces and hostages as the 'actors' and the world public, through the media – often 'live' on televison – as the appreciative 'audience'. A recent example was the TWA skyjack in June 1985 at Beirut, conducted in front of television cameras, at times seemingly almost solely for their benefit; it lasted nineteen days, the terrorists squeezing every ounce of publicity they could from the situation.

State Terrorism

When accused, terrorists point to the other side of the coin and in turn accuse governments of using state terrorism against them, often with justification. It is probably true that most liberal democratic governments try to 'fight clean', but few, if any, are able to achieve this ideal. Faced with a terrorist problem, such governments are compelled to pass anti-terrorist legislation to curb, and try to crush it. At the moderate end of the scale of response is arrest and detention without trial, banning of demonstrations and marches, imposition of curfews and issuing the security forces with CS gas and plastic bullets. Under terrorist provocation, security forces become more aggressive and occasionally exceed their brief, taking on covert operations with only assumed authority. Liberal democracies tend to become authoritarian too.

At the other end of the scale, totalitarian states faced with a terrorist problem or an insurgency go to extremes, using capital punishment, arbitrary arrests and concentration camps, while their counter-terrorist security forces hit back in kind, using death squads, forcibly removing sections of the population and razing villages. In such a situation individuals tend suddenly to 'disappear'. For example, since the authoritarian regime came to power in Guatemala some thirty years ago, according to Amnesty International, more than '88,000 people have disappeared'. Government death squads have been active in El Salvador, Guatemala and the Philippines. In some countries, mass graves are occasionally discovered, containing tortured bodies, the gruesome evidence of real state terrorism.

The Soviet Union, with its closed society, uses harsh methods too, sending dissidents to gulags (forced labour camps), into hospital psychiatric wards or internal exile, which usually means banishment to Siberia. A black blot on modern history was the welter of repression carried out in Iran immediately after the Khomeini regime came to power in 1979, which included the arbitrary execution of generals, officials, politicians and supporters of the ousted Shah. Stories ever since of execution and torture in Tehran's notorious Evin Prison, continue to trickle out to a scarcely believing public in the West.

Dirty Tricks Brigades Some nations have what is virtually a 'dirty tricks brigade', an overseas extension of their security forces secretly to combat terrorist elements beyond their normal legal reach. One of the most prominent of these is the Israeli Mossad secret service, which has gained notoriety for its covert exploits against enemies of the state, mainly Arab terrorists – but not always. In October 1986, Mordechai Vanunu, an Israeli nuclear technician, was snatched from Rome by Mossad, and whisked off to Israel, there to stand trial for leaking Israeli nuclear secrets to the London media.

In Cyprus, on 14 February 1988 a bomb killed three PLO senior officials, who were organizing a ship in which Palestinians who had been deported from Israel were to make a 'symbolic re-entry into Israel'. On the 15th, an explosion holed the ship, causing the project to be abandoned. It bore all the hallmarks of Mossad, as did the commando night raid on the Tunis HQ of the PLO on 17 April 1988, which killed Abu Jihad, deputy leader of the PLO, who was in charge of its military activities, and had been accused of organizing the Uprising (Intifada) in the occupied West Bank territories.

France has its Direction Général de la Sécurité Etranges (DGSE), or overseas intelligence service. In July 1985 in a New Zealand harbour, DGSE operatives stuck limpet mines on a Greenpeace ship, which sank it, killing a crew member in the process. At the time Greenpeace was campaigning against French nuclear testing in the Pacific area.

Britain has its Special Air Service Regiment (SAS), which has been accused of crossing the border illegally into the Republic of Ireland; they wage a dangerous covert war in Ulster against the IRA and recently shot an IRA unit operating in Gibraltar. The US Central Intelligence Agency (CIA), perhaps the most publicized secret service in the world, snatched a terrorist from a private yacht in the

Mediterranean and spirited him to the USA for trial. According to some accounts, the CIA has had many failures in its attempts to kill enemies of the state, including Colonel Gaddafi of Libya. Just a few years ago it was involved in a failed attempt to kill a Hezbollah leader in Beirut by car bomb; it failed, causing great loss of life to bystanders. It is alleged that the CIA also organized a terrorist bomb explosion at a press conference in Costa Rica in March 1984 that killed five innocent people, but the target person, Eden Pastora ('Captain Zero'), a Sandiniste, who turned his coat to become a CIA-backed 'Contra' but had refused to work with Contra ex-Samozan Republican Guards, escaped with a slight wound.

Libyan death squads roamed the capitals of western Europe in the mid-1980s, seeking out Gaddafi's enemies who had ignored his order to return home. The Soviet KGB is depicted in sinister colours, and many crimes are ascribed to it, especially by novelists; but it seems to concentrate mainly on espionage and counter-espionage. Accusations of its involvement in international terrorism are many, but proof seems to be lacking.

State-Aided Terrorism Some states aid external terrorism with the objective of destabilizing hostile countries and embarrassing unfriendly governments. Prime examples are Libya, Syria and South Yemen, which have long provided sanctuary, training camps for terrorists, arms and money. The emphasis was at first mainly against Israel, but as international terrorism developed, American and Western targets anywhere in the world were attacked. Also, Palestinian terrorist groups raided into Israel, with the connivance of adjacent Arab states.

Embassies and consulates of states that aid terrorism, have stored arms for terrorist use in west European and other capitals, issued false diplomatic passports, given terrorists 'new identities' and sanctuary. The British Government severed diplomatic relations with Syria, in April 1986 when its London Embassy produced an explosive device for an Arab to put on an Israeli airliner.

Some countries have given funds and covert help to terrorist groups active against their enemies, but have denied it officially. The Islamic Conference Organization (ICO) is alleged to have supplied both arms and money to the Muslim separatist group Moro National Liberation Front (MNLF) in the Philippines. Other states are accused of allowing terrorist groups to operate from their soil; while they strongly deny the fact, fingers point to the Republic of Ireland, France and certain Arab countries.

Third World Conflicts A number of struggles currently in progress in Third World countries by resistance groups against alien, colonial or authoritarian governments are regarded as 'proxy' superpower wars with the USSR backing one side, and the West supporting the other. These include Angola, Afghanistan, Central American States, Kampuchea and Mozambique. The double standards of both superpowers stand out in this respect. There seem to be no universally accepted rules for what constitutes a freedom fighter as opposed to a terrorist. The Americans are supplying the Afghan Mujahideen with arms to use against Soviet troops in Afghanistan; and the Soviets, through the Cubans, are backing the Sandinista government of Nicaragua, fighting against the American-backed Contras; while in Angola the Western-backed National Union for the Total Independence of Angola (UNITA) is struggling against the Marxist Popular Movement for the Liberation of Angola (MPLA) government; the Cuban troops it employs on a mercenary basis are supported by the Soviet Union.

2. Euro-Terrorism International

'We are going through days of particular violence; Red and Black terrorism, and organized crime with its fights between factions – all this is spreading.' – Oscar Scalfaro: Italian Minister of the Interior (4 April 1985)

FTER the violent and bloody 1970s, when 'international terrorism' burst upon the world with its dramatic welter of skyjackings, hostage-taking, assassinations, bombings and shootings, it seemed at the turn of the decade that both its volume and momentum were declining, owing to improved anti-terrorism measures, public acceptance of certain restrictions like personal searches before boarding an aircraft, and the successes of security forces in capturing terrorists and their leaders and detecting caches of terrorist arms and explosives. Perhaps people were becoming hardened and indifferent to terrorist violence – a lax attitude of complacency that continued into the early 1980s, until it was rudely shattered.

The Year of Euro-Terrorism

AD-RAF Declaration On 15 January 1985, a joint Action Directe (AD)-Red Army Faction (RAF) Declaration stated that they were forming a 'Joint Military Front' to wage a 'western European Revolutionary Offensive' against the 'multi-national structure of NATO'. That year became one of 'Euro-Terrorism'. On 23 January, General Réné Audran, Head of French international arms sales, was shot dead as he arrived at his home on the outskirts of Paris, by two members of the 'Elizabeth van Dyck Commando' of Action Directe. An unknown caller had telephoned the General's house in the afternoon asking what time he would return, and was told exactly. A joint AD-RAF communiqué was sent to a media office in Paris claiming responsibility for the assassination, stating that 'Communist guerrilla warfare in western Europe' had begun. The French police, who had recently captured nineteen AD members and thought they had neutralized that organization, were taken by surprise. (Elizabeth van Dyck was an RAF 'martyr', killed in a shoot-out with West German police in May 1979.)

It had been the intention of the RAF to strike the first blow in this joint anti-NATO campaign on 21 January, but as RAF member Johannes Thimme and his woman companion Claudia Wanneradorfer wheeled a pram containing a timed explosive device into position in Stuttgart it exploded prematurely killing the man and severely injuring the woman.

However, the RAF were ready to strike on 1 February, when three members of the 'Patrick O'Hara Commando' shot dead Ernst Zimmermann, head of a firm that manufactured engines for military aircraft, in Munich. Zimmermann had answered his front door to a young woman who said she had a letter for him to sign: then her two male companions pushed their way into the house, tied up Zimmermann and his wife and killed him in cold blood. An AD-RAF communiqué claimed responsibility, stating that the victim had been 'executed'. West German police had been as complacent as their French counterparts, estimating that barely twenty RAF terrorists were still at large. (Patrick O'Hara was an INLA hunger-striker who died in a Belfast prison after 61 days without food, his name giving an international flavour to the incident.)

During the following months a series of small bomb attacks occurred in both France and West Germany, for which responsibility was claimed sometimes jointly but mostly individually by the indigenous group. Common factors were that both used the same type of explosive material, which had been stolen from a Belgian quarry.

France

France had its share of indigenous terrorist groups which had operated inter-mittently for some time. Often separatists, they ranged from the virile and violent Front de la Libération Nationale de la Corse (FLNC), demanding independence for the island of Corsica, to the more passive Front de la Libération de la Bretagne – Armée Républicaine (FLB-AR), which wanted an independent Brittany. A few others were right-wing ones, but most were of the opposite political persuasion; one of the most prominent, which became very active in the 1980s, was the left-wing Action Directe. Formed in 1979 by Jean-Marc Rouillon and Natalie Menignon as a legal political organization with a radical left-wing and anti-imperialist orientation, Action Directe commenced terrorist activity almost at once against a variety of targets, including Jewish ones. AD was funded by bank robberies, and one member (Neyer Azerouhalb) was later arrested in the act of committing one during which a man died; he was subsequently convicted of his murder. Within months however its two founder-members and some twenty others were in police detention.

The Tradition of Asylum The long French liberal tradition of granting asylum to persecuted exiles of many different nationalities and political persuasions attracted diverse refugees including those prepared to use violence to gain their goals. France's open society enabled terrorist groups to use that country as a battleground between themselves and against their own targets in the host country. It was often said that France tacitly gave freedom of residence and movement to terrorists in the unspoken expectation that they would abstain from violence in its territory – a far-fetched hope that did not materialize. In France, and in Paris particularly, Armenians attacked Turkish personnel and property; quarrelling Arab groups fought one another and the Israelis: the Israelis hit back; while left-wing anti-imperialist groups attacked American and NATO targets; and East European and Balkan exiled groups attacked Warsaw Pact and Balkan embassies and personnel, which in turn used state terrorism against them.

When François Mitterrand became President of France in 1981 he released all detained AD members in an amnesty, believing they were of little danger to the state. He also continued the French liberal sanctuary tradition, stating that France would not willingly extradite suspected terrorists 'if they are willing to renounce violence in return for asylum'. Most nations found the extradition process in France tedious and difficult, if not impossible. More than a dozen Red Brigades terrorists, wanted by the Italian authorities, were living openly in Paris and on 14 February 1985 Prime Minister Craxi of Italy said in the Italian Parliament that '120 extradition requests to France have been made, and none has been successful'.

After their release from detention, Action Directe members resumed their terrorist activity mainly around Paris. They aimed at countering 'NATO imperialist war preparation', and concentrated upon striking 'NATO-related targets'. AD also continued to strike at Jewish targets, and on 10 August 1982 four of its members sprayed bullets into a popular crowded Jewish-owned cafe in Paris, killing six people and injuring 22 others. The media dubbed this exploit the 'Jewish Restaurant Massacre'. On the 19th, Action Directe was proscribed; and on the 20th, twelve members were arrested. The remainder, perhaps a dozen or so, continued to attack a wide variety of targets during the following two years. AD members were occasionally sighted in Belgium, where on 3 February 1983, they caused explosions at the French Embassy and the Air France Office in Brussels.

Meanwhile the other terrorist organizations in France, especially smaller and less effective ones, were hungry for publicity too. Large or small, active or inactive, they all played up to the large international media presence in Paris. When an explosion occurred on 20 March 1982 on a Paris–Toulouse train, which killed five people and injured 27 others, five different groups claimed responsibility.

French Security Forces At the beginning of the decade, French police were barely able to contain the swarming groups of terrorists on their soil and were especially over-stretched by the myriad of small bombing attacks in Paris. Additionally, they had to provide protection for the main embassies, especially those of Iran, Israel, Turkey, the USSR, the United States and those of certain Arab countries.

French police were in two separate services. The para-military Gendarmerie Nationale (GN) under the Ministry of Defence, was about 80,000 strong, and had a nationwide remit to police the countryside, guard embassies and carry out 'special duties'. The Police Nationale, the uniformed civil policemen about 150,000 strong, came under the Ministry of the Interior, and was divided into the Police Parisienne (for Paris) and the Police Urban, to police towns with populations of more than 10,000 inhabitants. This also contained a para-military element, the Compagnies Républicaines de Sécurité (CRS). There was rivalry between the two police bodies, and co-operation between them was therefore not what it should have been. In September 1982 a new anti-terrorist team was formed, the Gendarmerie d'Intervention de la Gendarmerie Nationale (GIGN). Modernizing improvements were put in train.

In December 1982, the French Council of Civil Liberties finally gave its approval in principle to the installation of a central computer to store data on '60,000 terrorists and suspects', which was until then held on some 2,000,000 indexed cards. The new system was to have 52 terminals at ports, airports, frontier posts and main police stations so that information could be passed instantly and identity details checked out. The change-over was to be made in 1983, but terminals were slow to appear, cost being the retarding factor. In November 1984, in the National Assembly, the Minister of the Interior announced that the police were to be modernized, and money was voted for this purpose. He declared that the Police Parisienne was 'technically the worst equipped and developed in Europe'.

Action Directe activity continued over the months, and it was not until 21 February 1987 that the French police had their first big success against the organization, when they arrested the four main leaders in a remote farmhouse near Orléans. They were Jean-Marc Rouillon and Natalie Menignon, alleged to be jointly responsible for more than 80 bombing and shooting incidents since 1980; Joelle

Aubron, a 'poor little rich girl' from an upper class Parisienne family, who became a discontented drop-out; and Georges Cipriani, a 'hit-man'. An Action Directe supergrass, Joelle Crepet, jailed in 1986, had provided the police with information. Arms, documents and plans were all seized at the farmhouse, the often grandiose plans being of passing interest. One was to kidnap Willi Brandt, the former West German chancellor, who had a holiday home near Orléans, and to trade-exchange him for Regis Schleicher, a RAF member imprisoned in 1984 for the murder of two policemen in Paris. Another was to kidnap a named French senior nuclear scientist of the Atomic Energy Commission, and to extract from him the secrets of the neutron bomb. The French police announced on 22 March the discovery of a large cache of terrorist weapons (the sixth within weeks) and more AD arrests.

The four leaders, Rouillon, Menignon, Aubron and Cipriani, began a hunger-strike on 1 December and had to be carried into court for their trial, which began in January 1988. At the same trials 24 other Action Directe members were arraigned, of whom only nineteen were present, the remainder being tried in their absence: all were convicted. By this time it was thought all the activists at large had been arrested; an explosives expert, Max Frerot, captured in November, was considered to be the last one still on the run.

West Germany

In West Germany the 'first generation' of the notorious anarchist extremist Rote Armee Faktion (Red Army Faction or RAF), the 'Baader-Meinhof Gang' (so-called after its two founder-members, who had both committed suicide in the Stammheim maximum security prison at Stuttgart in 1976–7) which had caused so much fear and trembling since it first began to operate in 1968 was in 1980 struggling desperately to survive. Over half its leadership was either dead, in prison, in detention awaiting trial, on the run or hiding abroad. By 1980 the strength of the RAF, which had committed five murders, 55 'attempted murders' of people injured in explosions and countless minor bank robberies and bombings of buildings, was waning. At its zenith it had barely exceeded 70 activists.

The Federal Criminal Office Much of the credit for the success of the authorities against the RAF and other terrorist groups in West Germany must go to the Bundes-Kriminal-Amp (BKA), (Federal Criminal Office), whose special anti-terrorist 'target teams', each concentrating on tracking down one individual terrorist, had patiently, relentlessly and methodically reduced the 'Wanted: Top Terrorist' list from more than forty, to less than twenty. The BKA's most useful tool had been the anti-terrorist computer at Weisbaden, which had amassed some ten million pages of data on 'wanted terrorists', their habits and associates. Originally the computer had been established to trace stolen motor vehicles, but under the shadow of the RAF threat it had been expanded and rededicated without demur, despite being an infringement of civil liberties in such a liberty-conscious society.

Likenesses of suspected terrorists stared out from thousands of posters across the country, offering huge rewards for information leading to their capture. BKA determination had been demonstrated when in 1978 one of its anti-terrorist 'target teams' travelled to a Bulgarian Black Sea holiday resort, promptly and arbitrarily arrested four 'wanted' West German terrorists under the noses of the Bulgarian authorities, drove them to Burgas Airport and bundled them into a waiting

Lufthansa aircraft, which flew them to Cologne for trial. Another BKA success was chalked up in July 1980 when Knut Folkerts, an RAF leader who had been traced to Holland and extradited, was sentenced to life imprisonment for the murder (in April 1977) of Siegfried Buback, a Federal prosecutor.

As public apprehension subsided, there was official talk of the rehabilitation of hardened terrorists in return for repentance, the aim being to tempt the remaining fugitives to surrender. One example was Astrid Proll, a founder-member of the RAF, who had escaped to England and was working as a garage mechanic when arrested in 1978. She returned voluntarily to West Germany on the promise of a speedy trial and leniency. Granted bail while awaiting trial, after a nominal sentence had been passed, she was released. In August 1980, Horst Mahler, also an RAF founder-member, was released from prison. He had completely recanted and broken with his terrorist background. (As a lawyer, he later complained because he was not re-admitted to the Bar, and allowed to practise.)

The resurgence of German terror In early 1981 there was a series of hunger-strikes by imprisoned terrorists and those awaiting trial, protesting against harsh, solitary conditions. In some cases concessions were made. On 16 April, Sigurd Debus died after being on hunger-strike for 70 days, thus providing the 'hard left' with another martyr. A flurry of small bomb attacks followed, responsibility being claimed mainly by the Revolutionär Zellen (RZ), (Revolutionary Cells), a 'second generation' RAF organization with a maximum of 50 activists. The 'Martyr Debus' was unusual as he was really only a small-time, almost freelance terrorist who had concentrated on bank robberies and small explosions. He was not a member of either the RAF, the RZ, or the other formerly powerful left-wing terrorist group, the Bewegung 2 Juni (Second of June Movement), which operated in West Berlin, but had also lost most of its leadership and its momentum. The BKA estimated left-wing terrorist groups were down to about 100 activists, mostly small fry, with some 10,000 supporters and sympathizers.

Even reduced in size these groups could still act, and on 11 May 1981 Heinz Herbert Karry, the Hesse State Economic Minster, who had offered large rewards for information leading to RAF arrests, was shot dead at his home in Frankfurt. On 31 August a large bomb exploded at a car park at the US-NATO Air Force Operations HQ at Ramstein, injuring twenty people; and on 15 September a rocket attack was made on the car of General Krossen, commander of US troops in West Germany. The RAF claimed responsibility for these incidents against typical targets. President Reagan's visit to West Germany in June 1982 caused a rash of minor bomb attacks against American targets by both the RAF and the RZ – on one occasion eight widely separated incidents occurred in one night. Small bombing attacks continued intermittently, but did not usually cause any casualties. In 1982 the BKA logged 184 such incidents.

During 1983 and 1984, terrorist attacks continued against American and NATO targets. Several arrests were made, many of individuals not on the wanted lists, some not even known to the police. This surprised the BKA, which thought it had almost eliminated the 'hard-left' urban terrorist threat. Attacks on US military and civilian targets tended to increase in frequency, causing critical comments to be made about the BKA's complacency and lack of efficiency.

In October 1982, there was a change of government in West Germany, and the new Minister of the Interior, Friedrich Zimmermann, adopted a much harder line against terrorism, prodding the BKA into greater activity. In November, Adelheid Schultz and Brigitte Mohnhaupt, two top activists of the RAF (the latter being its ideologue), were arrested, and a few days later so was Christian Klar, a former science student and also a top activist. This left only about fifteen left-wing terrorist activists, including nine women, at large. The BKA confidentally believed it had broken the back of the RAF; and the police talked of having a 'sanitizing function for society'. That July, six more RAF members were picked up in Frankfurt, four of whose faces were on the ubiquitous wanted notices. (Carelessness had cost them their freedom, not police detection. One of them had accidentally discharged a loaded pistol, the 9mm bullet entering the apartment below. The occupant called the police.) Eventually, in April 1985, Klar and Mohnhaupt were each given 'five life sentences, plus fifteen years imprisonment'.

Growth of Neo-Fascism Glimpses of neo-Fascism were appearing in West Germany, and with them fear of anti-Semitic activity. One neo-Fascist organization, the Military Sports Group Hoffman, led by Michael Kuhen, was responsible for a bombing incident at the 1980 Munich Oktoberfeste in which fourteen people died, and also for placing bombs in the cars of American servicemen. Kuhen was arrested in June 1981, and other arrests made during the following months effectively neutralized the group. Two members, Walther Kexel and Ulrich Tillman, were extradited from Britain, Kexel later committing suicide in prison.

Terror through Co-operation After the January 1985 joint AD-RAF declaration, RAF terrorist activity continued in West Germany, some 51 attacks being made in the first four months on NATO-related targets, mostly small ones. A major exploit occurred on 6 June, when a bomb exploded at Frankfurt Airport, killing three people and injuring 42. Comments were made on BKA inefficiency – the RAF was coming to life again, as young, educated and dedicated people were being attracted to its cause, the so-called 'third generation', better organized into tight cells, and tending to look outwards into the rest of western Europe. Responsibility for some of the terrorist acts committed in West Germany was claimed by the Revolutionary Cells, which also was attracting youthful and eager recruits; the police estimated that its strength now exceeded 40.

At about 7.30pm on 8 August 1985, a bomb exploded inside the US Air Force Base at Frankfurt, killing two people and injuring seventeen; and a joint RAF-AD communiqué claimed responsibility. At about the same time, the body of an American serviceman from the base was discovered in the vicinity. He had been shot, and it was initially assumed there was no connection with the terrorist exploit; the fatality had occurred as the result of an affair with a local girl. However, on the 13th the Reuters office at Frankfurt received a parcel containing the dead serviceman's identification documents and a copy of the RAF-AD communiqué – the terrorist who had planted the bomb would have needed genuine identification means to enter the base. For days this information was kept secret by the US authorities, mainly for the sake of morale, since it was not thought wise to publicize the fact that terrorists would kill to obtain identity cards to enter American bases in West Germany.

During 1986 the RAF remained active, and on 9 July they killed Karl-Heinz Beckurte, head of an industrial firm near Munich, with a car bomb. The first terrorist assassination in Bonn, the Federal capital, occurred on 10 November, when Gerold von Braunmuhl, a senior foreign office official, was shot by masked gunmen upon returning to his home by taxi. The gun, a Smith & Wesson .38in revolver, was identified by the BKA as having also fired the shots that had killed Hans-Martin Schlayer, a West German industrialist, in 1977. This incident prompted the authorities to initiate a 'supergrass system' and also to increase rewards offered for information leading to the arrests of terrorists. In the case of von Braunmuhl the reward offered was almost $2,000,000.

According to BKA estimates, during 1987 the hard core of the new 'third generation' of the RAF had risen to more than 40 members still at large, with another 50 or so 'helpers', and 200 active sympathizers. The RAF continued to claim responsibility for numerous assassinations, explosions and sabotage of NATO-related targets. On 21 March at Rheindahlen, a bomb placed under a car near an officers' mess exploded, injuring 31 people. The same day, an RAF attempt to blow up a troop train, had failed.

A lull followed until September, when in West Berlin Judge Günther Korbmacher, who dealt with the granting of asylum for political refugees, was wounded by gunmen while leaving his apartment to walk to his adjacent garage. One of two terrorists waiting on a motorcycle shot the judge in the leg at close range as a 'punishment' – a method copied from the Irish Republican Army (IRA). Responsibility was claimed by the RZ.

The BKA was of the opinion that the RZ was involved in a 'structural debate', trying to move away from the 'occasional blind actionism' to replace it with 'meaningful revolution'. After the 'comparatively quiet period', the BKA was expecting an 'autumn of blind terrorism' in West Berlin. In the event, this did not materialize.

Portugal

The AD-RAF declaration, which had signalled the commencement of Euro-Terrorism, had been preceded by a series of secret meetings in Portugal during 1984, sponsored by the Forcas Populares 25 de April (FP-25), a group that wanted to develop European links. By the end of that year it claimed to have been responsible for twelve assassinations, more than 200 bombing incidents, and 40 bank robberies. Terrorist leaders from Belgium, France, Holland, Greece and West Germany were invited to these meetings, and they all agreed to work on a master plan for attacking NATO-related targets.

Forcas Populares 25 de April The formation of FP-25 had been somewhat unusual. It took its title from the date of the Portuguese Revolution, 25 April 1974, when a left-wing military *coup* toppled a right-wing dictatorship. The operational commander of the *coup* had been Colonel Otelo Saravia de Carvalho, who had immediately become a national hero. Another military *coup* by more politically moderate officers was successful in November 1975, when Otelo was pushed aside to become an unsuccessful contender in the 1976 presidential election. In June 1980 he formed the Forcas de Unidade Popular (FUP), a front of seven radical left-wing groups from which Communists were excluded. Otelo was again unsuccessful in the 1980 presidential election. However, at the same time he had also formed FP-25 as a secret military arm of the FUP, recruiting young malcontents from the unemployed in industrial areas. FP-25 embarked upon a campaign of bank robberies, two policemen being killed in one such exploit, arson and bombing activities. This was extended to land-owners and industrialists who were in the process of recovering their property from state ownership, especially if they had treated their workers harshly; and at least one was assassinated. Initially FP-25 reputedly obtained some help from Libya and also claimed to have contact with the Basque ETA and the Italian Red Brigades and Prima Linea groups.

Otelo decided to intensify FP-25 activities and to place it firmly on the European terrorist map. On 20 April 1984 his organization exploded 110 small bombs across the country, some of which released pamphlets outlining his manifesto. His plan, it proclaimed, was to prevent the return of Fascism by 'forming a revolutionary army to overthrow the capitalist dictatorship', and to 'return power to the people'. The now-alerted authorities took action, and on 19 June Otelo and several FP-25 activists were arrested. Intensive police activity continued in the following weeks. On 10 August, Jeao Carlos Correla, the FP-25 'Northern Commander' was also captured, being the 43rd member to be detained, and several caches of arms and incriminating documents were discovered.

The Portuguese Government now thought they had crushed FP-25, whose maximum strength had never been more than about 120 activists; but even though its main leadership had been captured and the ranks depleted, the group was still able to contribute to the anti-NATO campaign. On 15 October 1984, it made five bomb attacks on French property in Lisbon, including a bank; on 25 November it fired grenades at the United States Embassy; and on 9 December it fired some small mortar bombs, which hit the HQ building of the NATO South Atlantic Command, at Oeiras. In most cases damage was done, but no serious casualties were incurred.

In January 1985 FP-25 was continuing to operate; it managed to fire several mortar bombs at NATO warships in the Tagus estuary, all of which missed their targets; and on 1 February bomb attacks damaged vehicles at the West German Air Force training base at Beja, in southern Portugal. FP-25 warnings were given to the Portuguese Government for it to withdraw these NATO facilties.

Supergrass Trials In October 1984, Otelo and 77 others had been charged with a variety of terrorist crimes. When the mass trial finally began on 22 July 1985, only 54 defendants were present in court, the remainder being tried in their absence. A purpose-built maximum security court house had been constructed for the trial at Monsanto, outside Lisbon, with bullet-proof partitions shielding judges, court officials, witnesses and defendants, and an iron cage ready to envelope the defendants should the presiding judge think it necessary. The accused all wore a red carnation, the symbol of the 1974 Revolution. A dramatic event occurred shortly before the trial opened when a supergrass (Jose Manuel Barradas) was fatally shot by an FP-25 activist. Barradas was not to die until August but the shooting held up the trial for a while and served as a warning to others who might be tempted to talk. Five other supergrasses were already being kept separately in protective custody. Ten of the prisoners escaped from custody in October; and then the Director of Prisons himself was assassinated by an FP-25 gunman on 15 February 1985. The trial did not end until 19 May 1987, when Otelo was found guilty of founding and leading a terrorist organization. He was sentenced to imprisonment; sixteen defendants were acquitted; and the remainder were given prison sentences.

The barely surviving FP-25, which had helped at the birth of Euro-Terrorism, was now unable to contribute in any significant degree to its growth. With its original leadership behind bars, some 40 or so survivors struggled to keep the FP-25 alive and active, and, although during 1987 its members carried out a few minor exploits and explosions, the momentum seemed to have gone from the organization. That year a new terrorist group appeared calling itself the Armed Revolutionary Organization, which began to claim responsibility for bombing incidents. As yet, little is known about it, but some sources feel it is a 'second-generation' rising from the ashes of the old FP-25.

Belgium & Holland

In Belgium, the Cellules Combattants Communistes (CCC), a small terrorist group, quickly associated itself with the AD-RAF declaration, having been involved in the discussions that led to it. Belgium had been comparatively free from terrorist problems, especially indigenous ones. Perhaps the most serious exploit was an explosion at a synagogue in Antwerp on 20 October 1981, which killed two people and injured 95. Authorities are undecided as to which organization was responsible; some thought it was the Armed Arab Struggle, led by Carlos 'the Jackal'; others pointed the finger at the PFLP-GC, led by Ahmad Jabril; but no one seemed absolutely sure.

The CCC, a previously unknown terrorist group, appeared in October 1984 to carry out a few small bombing attacks on government buildings. On 4 December, it caused five widely spaced explosions on the vulnerable, but vital, underground NATO fuel pipeline system, which extends some 3,680 miles to supply forward airfields and which runs through Belgian and West German territory. They also claimed responsibility for explosions in cars outside the SHAPE HQ.

The leader and founder of the CCC was Pierre Carette, an Action Directe member. Most of the group's exploits were carried out at night, after warning had been given, against NATO-related targets or Belgian government buildings, with occasional sabotage of the NATO fuel pipeline system; and consequently few casualties were caused. The CCC used explosives identified as being stolen from a Belgian quarry; the same materials were used in devices claimed to have been placed by AD and RAF. The CCC claimed its fifteenth attack on 1 May 1985 when a car bomb exploded outside the Belgian Employers' Federation building in Brussels, killing a fireman and nine other people. Just before the blast, men were seen near the vehicle, handing out leaflets stating that the car was booby-trapped and warning everyone to keep clear of it. Fire service personnel had been called, but, unaware of the warning and believing the vehicle to be on fire, they rushed forward, only to meet the full force of the bomb.

Five separate incidents occurred on 4 November for which the CCC said it was responsible. In one, terrorists ambushed a postal van carrying money, immediately blasting it open while two postal workers and one policeman were still inside. The postal workers were killed and the policeman injured; another policeman was taken hostage by the terrorists, who then drove off in the van, which contained about $120,000. The police hostage was later dumped by a roadside.

The Belgian authorities had been completely taken by surprise. The Government had long operated a 'soft' policy towards foreign terrorists on its soil by ignoring them as far as possible provided they remained inactive. The police had no specially trained teams to deal with them, and Groupe de Répression du Terrorisme (GRT) was hastily formed. It quickly obtained its first success on 18 December 1985 when it arrested Pierre Carette and three other armed CCC members at Namur. After its leader's arrest, the momentum of the CCC tended to decrease, although it still carried out small exploits. During 1987 the GRT teams were getting into their stride, capturing more than 25 CCC members; this left only about a dozen at large, who still made the occasional 'needling' anti-NATO attacks and a few sabotage attempts on the NATO fuel pipeline system.

The outbreaks also affected the Netherlands, where a by-now familiar pattern ensued. The police HQ and defence buildings at Groningen were bombed in January 1985, the previously unknown Northern Terror Front claiming responsibility for the act. However, suspicions were being aroused among Europe's security forces that the CCC were involved in the spate of operations, for there were a number of common factors: they were small bomb attacks with warnings, aimed at NATO-related and host-government buildings; they were frequently at night; and the explosives used in each case came from the same Belgian quarry. As if to confirm the theory, little has been heard of the Dutch group since.

Greece

Another country where terrorists associated themselves with the Joint AD-RAF declaration, and so in theory at least joined the Euro-Terrorism coalition, was Greece, which had gained an unenviable reputation of being a crossroads and staging-post for international terrorists – where those on the run could be re-equipped with new identities and travel documents. Most major international terrorist organizations had representatives in Athens, an allegation the Greek Government strenuously, but unconvincingly, denied. Athens Airport had become notorious for its lax security and poor anti-terrorist measures, it being said that skyjackers and their weapons were often able to slip aboard aircraft there. Certainly, a number of skyjacks began after a stop-over call at Athens, causing complaints by various airline pilots' associations. Greek governments were sympathetic towards the Arabs, and specifically the Palestinian cause, which perhaps often influenced their actions as they adopted a benevolent attitude towards terrorists in the usual forlorn hope that they would be suitably grateful and leave them alone.

November 17 Group   The main indigenous terrorist organization in Greece was the November 17 Group, which had an anti-Western platform. It was named after that date in 1973, when a student uprising began against the then ruling military junta. Its first major exploit was to assassinate the CIA station chief in Athens (Richard Welch). By the end of 1985 it claimed to have killed two Americans and seven Greeks. It specialized in political murders and usually left political pamphlets at the scene of the crime. One such incident was on 15 November 1983, when a US naval officer (Captain George Tsantes) was killed when his car stopped at traffic lights – two terrorists on a motor cycle drew up alongside his car and shot him with a .45in magnum pistol. (Cars of foreign diplomats in Greece had green number plates, and that of an ambassador always ended with the figure '1', making diplomats easily identifiable targets for would-be assassins.)

The November 17 Group also carried out bombing attacks against buildings, and on one day exploded six bombs in Athens. It claimed responsibility for an explosion on 3 February 1985 at a bar in Glyfada, near Athens, that was frequented by US servicemen; it injured 78 people, mainly Americans. This was claimed as a protest 'against the attitude of the US Administration towards the Cyprus situation'. On the 21st of that month, three terrorists from November 17 walked over to a car in an Athens street, in which a publisher sat, and shot him dead. They did not even bother to cover their faces, but simply walked away. The subsequent statement of admission alleged that the victim was working for the CIA.

In March 1985 the November 17 Group issued a manifesto announcing its unification with the AD, CCC and RAF and supporting the aims of the January declaration. Among their subsequent exploits was an explosion on 8 August at an Athens hotel, where British tourists stayed; fourteen people were injured. The Group alleged that it was a British spy-centre. On another occasion, on 26 November, it caused an explosion by remote-control in a bus taking policemen to their posts in Athens. One man died and twelve others were injured.

Other minor terrorist organizations operated in Greece, one of which was the Revolutionary Group of International Solidarity: Cristos Kassimis, also with a strong anti-American bias, which in March 1985 claimed responsibility for a large bomb discovered outside the West German Embassy in Athens, but which was safely defuzed. (Cristos Kassimis was a 'martyr' who had been killed by Greek police in 1977 during the Group's attack on a West German installation.) The November 17 Group activated another bomb on 24 May 1987 on a bus carrying US servicemen to the US Air Base at Hellenikon, injuring 17 of them. In July the United States yet again condemned the Greek Government for its 'soft, intransigent' attitude towards terrorism and for allowing an Arab terrorist (Abu Nidal) to open an office in Athens. The Greeks regarded this criticism as 'political sabotage'.

Italy

While in West Germany, for example, a comparatively small number of terrorists had badly shaken the nation, in Italy terrorism, kidnapping for ransom, organized crime, and Mafia activities had become an almost acceptable, although terrible, way of life. None of the Italian terrorist groups showed any interest in Euro-Terrorism, or the AD-RAF declaration, being of parochial character and fully involved in activities in their own country. During 1980, in which 1,264 'terrorist-related incidents' were recorded, the Italian Ministry of the Interior admitted it did not know exactly how many terrorist groups were operating in the country, making a guess that there were just over 130, of which it was thought one-fifth were neo-Fascist or right-wing, the remainder being of left-wing persuasions, some of which were little more than gangs of thugs dominating neighbourhoods, mixing crime and politics for their own gain. The Ministry of the Interior spokesman added that there were probably more than 10,000 active terrorists in all, with perhaps in excess of 100,000 supporters and helpers. This situation had come about owing to a variety of causes that included weak government continually composed of coalitions and a combination of lethargy, rivalry and lack of co-operation between the several police forces and government security agencies. Anti-terrorist training, suitable equipment, expertise and conditioning were also wanting.

The Red Brigades Out of this welter of terrorist groups, the strongest and most effective by far was the radical left-wing Brigate Rosse (Red Brigades or RB), which was active in all the main cities. Its structure was based on 'twin non-communicating cells', each of up to half-a-dozen individuals, controlled by 'cell commanders', answerable to 'brigade commanders' who in turn were answerable to the 'column commander' – each level (in theory) being sealed off from the others. This tight cell system was designed to maintain maximum security, and if members were arrested and interrogated they would be liable to divulge only limited information.

The Red Brigades' Strategic Command decided policy, but column commanders had latitude in implementing it. In 1980 there were sixteen RB columns, usually known by the names of their localities, although some adopted names of 'martyrs'. Nationwide the strength of the RB was probably just over 1,000 activists (no one knows exactly), the Rome Column, for example, having about 100 terrorists. Money was raised from bank robberies and kidnapping for ransom, while weapons were either captured from the security forces or given by the Palestine Liberation Organization (PLO). Certain Red Brigades personnel had been trained in camps in east European countries.

On 12 December 1980 the Rome Column of the RB kidnapped Giovanni D'Urso, a minor judge who controlled the movement of prisoners between maximum security jails, and held him in a 'people's prison' hideout where he was 'tried' and condemned to death. The judge was offered his freedom if the media would publish certain Red Brigades communications; they also wanted a video cassette of D'Urso's 'interrogation and trial' to be shown on televison. The Red Brigades wished to obliterate some of the smears and allegations of criminality and improve the image of its 'political integrity'. The Government, which had banned terrorist communications being used by the media, refused to negotiate. Eventually, however, one magazine risked official reprobation and published extracts, and Judge D'Urso was released safely.

The following year, on 17 December, US General James Dozier, Deputy Chief of Staff at the US Base in Verona, was kidnapped by members of the Red Brigades Verona Column posing as plumbers, the General being the first non-Italian to suffer this fate. Dozier was taken to a 'people's prison' near Padua and held for 45 days until forcibly rescued on 26 January 1982 by a 6-man armed anti-terrorist team, which accomplished a dawn rescue in 90 seconds, capturing five terrorists in the house. A bulldozer had been brought in to work nearby to drown any give-away noises from the rescue team. This was a major triumph for the Italian security forces, which were just re-organizing and re-training to meet the terrorist threat.

The Pentiti The Government now instigated an increasingly familiar counter-terrorist tactic: a supergrass system. They aimed to build up a detailed intelligence picture by encouraging imprisoned and detained members to become informers, or 'pentiti' (penitents), in return for lenient treatment. For several months this worked well, many terrorist leaders and activists being captured, or killed in police shoot-outs. The pentiti were usually very co-operative, and police spokesmen continually commented triumphantly that they all 'sang like canaries'. Indeed, Dozier's rescue had been achieved with information obtained in this way, and in its aftermath 340 terrorists were arrested and 45 hideouts were discovered. Those arrested included the commander of the Milan Column, Mario Moretti; the Tuscany Column's leader, Umberto Calabiani; and two members of the organization's Strategic Command, Marcello Capuano and Giovanni Senzani. Before he went underground in early 1981, Senzani had been a Professor of Criminology at Padua University, adviser to the

Government on prison conditions, and a Roman Catholic 'peacenik', who demonstrated against the American military presence in Vietnam. Differences had arisen within the Red Brigades between 'militants' who wanted more terrorist activity and the 'politicals' who wanted a greater political emphasis. Taking advantage of this controversy, Senzani had been about to make his bid for supreme leadership when in January 1982 he was arrested in his apartment in Rome, where arms, plans and other incriminating evidence were found.

The productive Pentiti system suddenly dried up when Roberto Peci, an electrician and a Red Brigades informer, was detected by his comrades, kidnapped, tortured and killed. This had a dampening effect, generally discouraging informers; and eventually in mid-1983 the Government terminated the system, declaring, 'It has served its purpose.' In fact it had not, and the Government later resurrected the scheme when it passed legislation allowing for reduced sentences for the contrite and helpful.

As a result of the effectiveness of the informer system during the first years of the decade, a series of mass terrorist trials were held in Italy. These became both spectacles and vehicles for terrorist propaganda, but did give some satisfaction to the security forces, whose morale improved as heavy prison sentences were handed out. Although these show trials attracted immense publicity, terrorism in Italy was generally overshadowed by the Mafia crime syndicates, such as the notorious Camorra of Naples, and political intrigue. One of the first mass trials was of 40 Brigades members, including Mario Moretti, accused of involvement in the kidnapping and murder of the former Prime Minister Aldo Moro in 1978. Defendants were packed together behind bars inside metal cages in the court room.

Meanwhile terrorist activites contined dispite the arrests, and in February 1986 terrorists killed a former mayor of Florence and also tried to kill an aide of Prime Minister Craxi. The following year in March they killed General Licio Giorleri, Head of Aeronautics and Space Armaments, who was shot by men on a motor cycle while sitting in the back of his official car during the evening rush hour traffic. By the end of 1987 the Red Brigades were thought to be down to about 40 activists, who kept in touch with their former leaders, serving long sentences in prison, by means of the underground grapevine. Other groups still existed. One such smaller, but nevertheless important terrorist group was the left-wing Prima Linea (Front Line or PL), which operated in Milan, Florence, Genoa and Turin and was connected with the Red Brigades. In February 1980 its founder-leader, Maurice Bignomi, was captured in the act of robbing a jeweller's shop in Turin, and thereafter many other members were arrested. The security forces claimed that by the end of 1981, they had 'dismantled' Prima Linea, only to be unpleasantly surprised when some of its survivors sprang three of its leading women activists from a prison near Padua. One of the first mass trials to be held included 78 Prima Linea terrorists.

Another mass trial was that of 71 members (including eleven women) of the left-wing intellectual 'April 7 Group', led by Antonio Negri, a former professor. These terrorists (several in their absence) were convicted of plotting armed insurrection and were given prison sentences totalling more than a thousand years. Negri himself had been arrested in 1979, then released in 1983 after his election to the Italian Parliament as a representative of the Radical Party. He fled the country when his parliamentary immunity was suspended, to live openly in Paris – all Italian applications for his extradition being ignored by the French.

Fascist Terror and the Bologna Bombing Two bombs exploded on the Naples–Milan express train on 23 October 1983 just as it was entering a tunnel, causing fifteen deaths and injuring 115 people. Eight separate terrorist groups claimed responsibility for this atrocity, including the small left-wing extremist Nuclei Armati Proletari (Armed Proletariat Nucleus or NAP), and some right-wing ones such as the New Order and the Black Order. The Black Order had been involved in a similar type of exploit in much the same place in 1974; but, on this occasion two members (Franco Albanaini and Francisco Bumbaca) of the right-wing National Revolutionary Front were arrested and charged with the crime.

Early in 1987, in Rome, the long-awaited show trial began of nineteen men and one woman accused of implications in Europe's worst-ever terrorist outrage – the Bologna Railway Station bombing in 1980, which left 80 people dead and hundreds injured. The charge was coupled with a previous incident in Milan (in December 1979) in which eighteen people had been killed and many wounded. The Milan incident had become known as the 'Plaza Fontana Massacre'. The defendants were mostly neo-Fascists, together with a few Government secret service agents, the latter being accused of conspiracy to destabilize the country. Allegations of a cover-up and of attempting to subvert justice were made by defending lawyers. There had already been five investigations and eight Court hearings, without successfully identifying those responsible for the incidents – this was the ninth attempt. It was argued that neo-Fascist groups had deliberately targeted Bologna because it had a Communist local government, and Italy was a NATO country; other theorists claimed that the perpetrators were either *agents provocateurs*, or the Red Brigades themselves, who intended to incite a right-wing backlash.

One of the defendants was Stejane Delle Chiaie, who had been extradited from Venezuela, where he had been picked up in a drug-smuggling security sweep, and who was additionally charged with murder of an Italian judge. Another defendant was Luciano Petrone, who had been extradited from Britain in January 1983. Investigations had run a bizarre course, and at first an anarchist group, led by a female night club dancer, was blamed for both the Bologna and the Plaza Fontana explosions; then a suspect fell to his death from the upper floor of a police building in Milan, which inspired the author, Dario Fo, to write a highly successful play entitled *The Accidental Death of an Anarchist*.

The Middle East Invasion

During the 1980s the tentacles of Middle East terrorism reached into western Europe. One of the most active Middle East terrorist groups was the Fatah-Revolutionary Council (Fatah-RC), led by Abu Nidal, who specialized in indiscriminate international terror. In October 1980 his followers attacked the Copernic Street Synagogue in Paris, when four people died; in August 1981 they attacked a synagogue in Vienna, injuring two people; and in October 1982 they threw grenades and fired into a synagogue in Rome, killing a baby and injuring 34 other people. Abu Nidal's most significant exploit occurred in London on 3 June 1982, when his men attempted to kill the Israeli Ambassador, Shlomo Argov, who was shot and incapacitated. Three Fatah-RC terrorists were arrested by the British police, tried, convicted and sentenced to imprisonment for this crime. It was this incident that provided the catalyst provoking the Israelis into launching a military invasion into southern Lebanon, then a Palestinian sanctuary and hotbed of terrorism. It failed to deter acts in Europe though and in Greece, in March 1984, a lone Fatah-RC gunman fired five shots at British diplomat Kenneth Whitty, who was driving a car in Athens, killing him and wounding a passenger. The terrorist then turned and fired shots at the gathering crowd before calmly walking away. Abu Nidal claimed this was in retaliation for the arrest and imprisonment of his three terrorists in Britain, for shooting the Israeli Ambassador.

Abu Nidal Abu Nidal (Mohammed Sabri al-Banna), a Palestinian, was born in Jaffa, probably in 1939. His father was the prosperous owner of citrus plantations, but was dispossessed and evicted during the Arab-Israeli War of 1948–9. Abu Nidal was well educated, qualifying as an engineer at Cairo University, where he met the young Yasser Arafat and his colleagues. He became a founder-member of the Fatah group, led by Arafat, but eventually fell out with him and was expelled from the organization. He then formed his own break-away group named the Fatah-Revolutionary Council. Now violently anti-Arafat, he organized the assassination of Issam Ali Sartawi, a senior PLO member, in April 1983 in Portugal, and was condemned to death in his absence by Fatah. He kept up his feuding with Arafat and Fatah, and in July 1982 his terrorists killed the PLO Representative in Paris, Fadi Dani, who was the ninth senior PLO leader to be killed in that city in ten years, responsibility being usually divided between Abu Nidal and the Israeli Mossad.

Abu Nidal was more an organizer and director of terrorism than an active master terrorist, who gathered around him up to 200 dedicated, trained and conditioned 'Palestinian Martyrs', so-called even while still alive, whose services were often sought for state terrorism by Libya, Syria, Iraq and perhaps other countries too. No evidence is available that he ever actually took part in any of the exploits he organized, or ever personally killed any one. He became an elusive, shadowy figure, around whom legends flourished. Only one rather fuzzy photograph of him (circa 1974) exists on intelligence files. He deliberately 'played dead' in 1983–4 during a period of bitter PLO in-fighting to avoid the attention of Arafat's gunmen; and more recently rumours abound of his having had cosmetic surgery in some east European country. Known to suffer from a heart complaint, he probably had a heart by-pass operation, perhaps in late 1984, again reputedly in an east European country. Active again after his surgery, Abu Nidal instigated exploits in 1985 that included an attack on the British Airways Office in Madrid during July, killing one person and injuring 24 others; and another at a hotel in Athens in September, where a group of handicapped British children were staying – grenades were thrown into the swimming-pool, killing two people and injuring nine.

On 23 November 1985 an Egyptian passenger airliner with 92 people aboard took off from Athens Airport for Cairo. Once airborne, five skyjackers of Fatah-RC demanded the plane be re-routed to Malta. In the initial brief scuffle one skyjacker was killed and a security guard injured. On landing at Luqa Airport, Malta, a few passengers were released – but once they were down on the tarmac they were shot at by the terrorists, one passenger being killed and four others injured. Britain, the United States and France offered the Maltese Government the use of their anti-terrorist teams, but these offers were refused. Instead, the following day the Egyptian Saiqa (Storm) Commando arrived, and immediately stormed the aircraft. In an excess of zeal, 60 people were killed, the majority being passengers. Only one terrorist survived. (The Egyptian Saiqa Commando has an unfortunate record: in

1977 it intervened in a skyjack situation in Cyprus that ended in a fire-fight with the Greek Cypriot police, resulting in fifteen Egyptian commando deaths.) The skyjackers had leaflets on them stating that they belonged to the 'Egyptian Revolution', which was Abu Nidal's code-name for this particular operation. It had been carried out by his 'Palestinian Martyrs' on behalf of Colonel Gaddafi of Libya, then in sharp confrontation with Egypt. The Egyptian Government openly blamed Greece for lax security measures at Athens Airport and even hinted at Greek Government connivance.

However, Abu Nidal's major exploits during 1985 were the almost simultaneous attacks on the international airports at Vienna and Rome on 27 December. At Vienna Airport three of his terrorists opened fire with Kalashnikov automatic weapons on the EL Al check-in desk, killing three passengers and injuring more than 30. The terrorists momentarily escaped – a police car chase followed, and then a gun-battle, in which the police killed one terrorist and captured the other two (Tanfik Ben Chaovali and Mongi Saadouni), both of whom were eventually brought to trial in Austria and convicted. At Rome Airport, four of Abu Nidal's gunmen threw grenades into a coffee bar and then fired their Kalashnikovs at passengers queuing at the El Al and TWA check-in desks, killing thirteen people and injuring another 70. In the ensuing battle with the police, in which Israeli Mossad agents took part, three terrorists were killed, and the other wounded. The survivor, Ibrahim Khalid, was eventually brought to trial in Italy (although not until January 1988) and convicted. All seven terrorists had leaflets on them declaring that they were 'Palestinian Martyrs'; that 'war against NATO imperialism had begun'; and that they were members of the 'Arab Guerrilla Cells', a new 'revolutionary suicide commando'.

According to police sources, the survivors talked freely, stating that they had been trained in Lebanon, had reached their respective destinations by way of Damascus and Yugoslavia, and that the plan in both cases had been to kill, take hostages, seize aircraft, fly to Israel and crash the plane on Tel Aviv. Once again, Gaddafi had provided the money and Abu Nidal the expertise and 'Martyrs'.

The American CIA, which had previously warned that Abu Nidal's terrorists would attack west European airports, produced (2 January 1986) a list of 60 terrorist incidents in the previous two years which they claimed had been organized by Abu Nidal with Libyan money and support. The Israelis went one better, producing a similar list of more than 100 incidents in 'eleven different countries'. International tension remained high throughout January 1986 as American warships and combat aircraft sabre-rattled off the Libyan coast.

Abu Abbas Abu Nidal was not the only entrepreneur on the terrorist scene. Another was Abu Abbas (Mohammed Abu Abbas), leader of the Palestine Liberation Front (PLF), part of the PLO coalition, whose exploits did not always go according to plan. On 7 October 1985 four of his terrorists were travelling aboard the *Achille Lauro*, an Italian cruiser liner sailing from Alexandria towards Port Said. They had boarded as 'tourists' at Athens, and were in their cabin when a steward entered unexpectedly – to find them cleaning their Kalashnikovs. Had they not forgotten to lock their cabin door, this exploit might have taken a very different turn. Once discovered, the terrorists panicked, spraying bullets almost at random and wounding a sailor as they took over the ship, and ordered the captain to sail for the Syrian port of Tarsus. Fortunately, the majority of tourists on this cruise had disembarked at Alexandria to make the land trip to see the Pyramids and Cairo, planning to rejoin the ship at Port Said, and the few Israeli passengers had all left the vessel. The terrorists demanded that the Israelis release 50 Palestinian prisoners in return for the safety of the ship and all aboard. As no response came (except from Syria telling them that the ship would not be allowed into its waters), one elderly, disabled passenger, who by fate turned out to be Jewish, was shot and his body thrown overboard. Abu Abbas got in touch with his terrorists and ordered them to sail the ship towards Port Said.

There followed two days of high-level negotiations in Egypt between President Mubarak, Abu Abbas, Yasser Arafat (as Chairman of the PLO) and the ambassadors of the United States, Italy and Greece. The outcome was that the ship would be brought into Port Said and the terrorists would surrender to the Egyptian authorities in return for a safe conduct out of the country. (Only the American Ambassador demurred.) This was accomplished on the 9th. On the morning of the 10th, President Mubarak falsely told the American Ambassador that the terrorists had left Egyptian soil. Later that day, at almost midnight, four American F-14 combat aircraft, flying just south of Crete intercepted an Egypt Air Boeing 737, carrying the four seajackers and forced it to land at the US Base at Sigonelle in Sicily.

The Americans wanted to fly the terrorists to the USA, by way of an aircraft carrier, but the Italians insisted on taking the men into their custody. The Italians were able to arrest another accomplice in Italy, and in July 1986 at Genoa, the ship's home port, eleven terrorists involved in this exploit were tried and convicted, including Yusef Magied al-Molqi (who admitted killing the American passenger) and Abu Abbas (tried in his absence).

Further bad news for the Americans was that aboard the Egyptian airliner, much to their surprise, had been Abu Abbas himself! The Italians not only took him from them, but also quickly flew him off to Belgrade, dressed in the uniform of an Egyptian civil air pilot. President Mubarak, the Italians and the Greeks, had effectively collaborated with the terrorists.

The original Abu Abbas plan had been for his four terrorists to 'hitch a ride on the ship', to behave like normal tourists until it reached the Israeli port of Ashdod on its normal cruiser itinerary, where they were to massacre as many innocent people with their grenades and Kalashnikovs as possible. A PLF spokesman later said, 'The aim of the operation was not to hijack the ship, or its passengers . . . but to avenge the Martyrs of the Israeli raid on the PLO HQ [near Tunis].' This had been an Israeli long-distance air strike on 1 October 1985, which killed more than 65 people and injured more than 100. A senior PLO official stated, 'The men were under written orders from Abu Abbas to carry out a suicide mission in Ashdod, and they changed their minds out of cowardice when discovered, and instead decided to hijack the ship.' The last seajack within recent decades had been in 1960, that of the Portuguese liner *Santa Maria*, in protest against the country's dictatorial regime.

State Terror

Libya State terrorism left its bloody mark on western Europe during the 1980s. Colonel Gaddafi of Libya was a prime culprit, having about a hundred 'hit-men' touring Western capitals hunting down Libyan activists hostile to his regime. They also attacked other targets whenever opportunity offered. Libyan dissidents were executed by his teams in Athens, Bonn, London, Paris and Rome. The British expelled four Libyans in June 1980, and the Americans had temporarily to withdraw their ambassador from Paris in June 1981, as he was marked out as a target by Gaddafi. After bombs had exploded in London and Manchester in March 1984, injuring more than twenty people, three Libyans were convicted of terrorist offences and six more were expelled; while in Spain, in December 1985, three Libyan diplomats were expelled for similar reasons.

On 17 April 1984, during an anti-Gaddafi demonstration outside the Libyan People's Bureau in London, a British policewoman was shot dead by gunfire from within the building. The Bureau was besieged by security forces and eventually 32 Libyans were deported. That same month 22 Libyans were expelled from West Germany.

Iran Iran also practised state terrorism in western Europe. Its teams were especially attracted to Paris, the refuge of many Iranian exiles opposed to the Khomeini regime. A terrorist attempt had been made on the life of ex-Prime Minister Bakhtiar in July 1980; and an ex-Shahist General, Gholam Ali Oveissi, known as the 'Butcher of Tehran' for his methods of controlling anti-Shahist demonstrations, was shot dead in Paris in February 1984.

Syria That the Syrians were active too became evident when one of its operations failed in April 1986. A Palestinian terrorist working with the Syrians, Nazir Hindawi, tried to destroy an El Al airliner with 373 people on board by means of a timing device hidden in the luggage of his pregnant girl friend (Anne Marie Murphy) without her knowledge. Hindawi had promised to follow her to Israel to marry her, but fortunately the device was detected at London Airport before the girl boarded the aircraft. The British authorities firmly believed that the Syrians had not only known about this projected exploit in advance but had actively assisted in the operation. The explosive device had apparently been collected by Hindawi personally from the Syrian Embassy in London, which had also provided him with a false diplomatic passport.

This was a blatant example of callous terrorist indifference towards innocent victims. On the 18th, Hindawi and two accomplices were arrested in England, where they were eventually brought to trial and convicted. This attempted act of Syrian state terrorism was in retaliation for the Israeli interception of a Libyan aircraft in February 1986. Britain severed diplomatic relations with Syria; but many felt the real culprit was Colonel Gaddafi.

Nazir Hindawi was something of a terrorist entrepreneur, who just prior to his planned exploit in London, had organized an explosion that had occurred at about 2am on 5 April 1986 at the La Belle Discotheque in West Berlin, which was frequented by Americans; it killed two US Servicemen and a Turkish woman and injured 229 people, of whom some 60 were Americans. Responsibility was claimed by the West German Red Army Faction, but the United States reacted as it had long yearned to against Libya. They mounted an air strike against the Libyan cities of Tripoli and Benghazi on 15 April. Gaddafi and his family had narrow escapes, and an adopted child of his was among the dead.

Ahmad Hindawi (brother of Nazir) was arrested in West Berlin on 18 April and charged with involvement in the Berlin bombing. The discotheque explosion had been a joint Syrian–Libyan operation. Hindawi had brought the explosives from Damascus to East Berlin, taking them into the Syrian Embassy there; and he also probably carried them into West Berlin. The actual explosive device had been planted in the discotheque by Christine Endrigkeit, a West German RAF member who was to be arrested in January 1988. Nazir had carried out a previous bombing in West Berlin when an explosion at a meeting of the German–Arab Friendly Society on 9 August 1986 injured nine Arabs.

Carlos 'the Jackal' The shadow of Carlos 'the Jackal' (Ilyich Ramirez Sanchez), the master terrorist of the 1970s, briefly darkened western Europe. He had remained in the employment of his old paymaster, Colonel Gaddafi of Libya, and was elusively sighted in several countries, but in the early 1980s he came to rest temporarily in East Berlin, leading his Armed Arab Struggle group, which was mainly active in France. Two members of this group, Magdalena Kaupp, a West German, and Bruno Preguet, a Swiss, were arrested in Paris in February 1982 on their way to plant an explosive device – which, together with a number of domestic gas cylinders, arms and incriminating documents, was discovered in their car when stopped by the police.

Carlos wrote a short letter, in his own handwriting, which was given to the *Agence France-Presse* office in West Berlin, demanding their release and threatening a wave of terrorist violence if they were not set free. West Berlin police authenticated the handwriting as genuine and a thumb print on it to be that of Carlos. A number of explosions occurred in France for which the Armed Arab Struggle claimed responsibility. A bomb in a left-luggage office at Marseilles railway station exploded on 31 December 1983, killing two people and injuring fifteen; and on the same day there was an explosion on an express train from Marseilles to Paris, in which two people died and another nineteen were injured. Yet another handwritten letter from Carlos reached the West Berlin office of *Agence France-Presse*, claiming responsibility for those two outrages, and threatening more if his two detained members were not released. After he had made his last attempt to release his members, it is thought Carlos moved back to Libya. Later, in 1985, a senior Syrian intelligence officer told me that Carlos's days as an active terrorist were over, as he was neither physically nor mentally able to continue, having become quite obese through good living.

Europe's Anti-Terrorist Measures

In September 1986 the Interior Ministers of EEC countries met in London to discuss improved measures to combat terrorism. Sufficient documents had been seized, and other evidence obtained, to leave little doubt that Euro-Terrorism was a reality and not just a series of coincidences or causal liaisons; and that its continuing existence rested upon assistance from certain Middle East terrorist organizations. The Ministers formally declared war on Euro-Terrorism; identified 40 active terrorist groups in western Europe; named the twelve major ones, and produced a black list of some 200 terrorists who were to be hunted down relentlessly. Information about each terrorist activist at large was to be passed quickly between EEC countries, so that once sighted they could be tracked down and arrested. Technical snags existed: for example, the computers in Greece, Portugal and Spain were inferior to and incompatible with those in use in Britain, West Germany and Italy. The main complaint by the EEC Interior Ministers was that of internal inter-service rivalry and of difficulty in persuading these services not only to work with but also share information with each other and with external security services and agencies. Some countries had more than one security service with a police function: responsibilities were often divided between them, sometimes they overlapped, and sometimes there were gaps. A strong political leader was required in some national cases to merge security activities and to control them centrally – which was anathema to some statesmen, fearful of a totalitarian police state evolving if such powers were not divided, diluted and delvolved, to counter-balance one another. The French and German Governments had led the way on co-operation when, the previous year, they set up a telex hot-line to improve co-ordination and co-operation on terrorist issues.

Most EEC countries, except Britain and the Republic of Ireland, issued their citizens with some form of identity card or document, which they were to carry at all times. In late 1987, West Germany went one better by issuing a 'computer-readable identity card', and made plans to introduce a 'computer-readable passport' in 1988. This seemed to be merely keeping pace with terrorist expertise, as EEC policy was to ease cross-frontier controls between member countries (by 1992), and reduce the number of border check points, a policy of considerable help to terrorists but a hindrance to security forces attempting to track them down.

Euro-Terrorism International

Euro-Terror, as heralded by the AD-RAF coalition, had not been as serious a threat in reality as it had promised to be. Despite the emphasis placed on it by EEC Ministers, it had burst upon the scene, operated fitfully, faltered and faded. It had been overshadowed by the reappearance of Middle East terror with more sinister international links – 'Euro-Terror International' was far more serious.

3. The Hezbollah

These fanatical Shiites are typical of the newly militant Lebanese who are joining Islamic fundamentalist groups like the Hezbollah. The men are beating their heads, which they have cut with blades, as part of a demonstration during the Ashoura ceremonies in September 1985. Thousands of others joined them, beating their chests in penance for the martyrdom of Hussein, grandson of the Islamic prophet Mahomet. (Popperfoto)

'Ahmad Qassir is a Martyr of Islam' – Epitaph of a 16-year-old suicide truck-bomb driver,
Lebanon: 4 November 1983

The Rise of Militant Islam

I N Lebanon on 18 April 1983, a truck-bomb loaded with about 400 pounds of explosives, driven by a suicide-driver, crashed into the forecourt of the American Embassy in Beirut, to bump against the side-wall of the building, where it exploded, killing 63 people, including the CIA Director for the Middle East and six of his staff, and injuring 120 others. Responsibility was claimed by 'Islamic Jihad'. The driver was blown to pieces.

Car-bombs had long been a terrible feature of the Lebanese terrorist scene. They always gave the perpetrators a wide margin of personal safety and escape, since the terrorists had only to park the vehicle containing the bomb in position; it could then be detonated either by remote-control from some nearby secure hideout, or by a timing-device after the driver had made his getaway. The *kamikaze* attitude of the suicide-driver was a new aspect of terrorism, reflecting the fanaticism of the wave of 'Islamic Fundamentalism', loosely meaning 'militant Islam', sweeping through the Middle East in the wake of the Iranian revolution.

On 23 October the encampments of the American and French military peace-keeping contingents in the Multi-National Force (MNF), just south of Beirut, were attacked almost simultaneously by two vehicle-bombs. The truck driven at the American position, containing about 500 pounds of explosives, crashed through the perimeter wire fence into the lobby of the main building before the suicide-driver detonated his cargo, killing 241 US Marines. The American sentry on duty had fired his rifle at the approaching vehicle, but it did not stop. US Standing Orders that, in camp, weapons should not be loaded, prevented an instant barrage of small-arms fire which might have killed the suicide-driver, and so perhaps have halted the vehicle outside the camp area.

The other vehicle, carrying about 400 pounds of explosives, was driven head-on into a building housing a French military detachment, where it instantly exploded, killing 58 French troops. Both suicide-drivers, having been previously blessed by a Mullah, went willingly to their deaths, and so became 'Islamic Martyrs'. Responsibility was again claimed by Islamic Jihad; and in response, both American and French combat aircraft bombed camps in the Beka'a Valley, believed to be used for terrorist training.

A few days later another similar incident occurred, when a man drove his truck-bomb towards the Israeli HQ in Tyre (Lebanon). Although the vehicle stopped about five yards from the building, the Israelis having shot dead the driver with small-arms fire, the explosion set off a chain reaction of detonations within the Israeli compound as dumps of ammunition were successively ignited. It was some two hours before rescuers were able to get to work. The explosions killed 28 Israeli Servicemen and 35 Lebanese and Palestinians, some of whom were being inter-rogated. Responsibility was yet again claimed by Islamic Jihad, which stated through the local media that, 'We are prepared to send 2,000 of our fighters to die in Southern Lebanon in order to expel the Zionist enemy from our country.'

The terrible chain of events revealed the hate which had been aroused among many Lebanese in the wake of the Israeli invasion of their country. The latest driver had been 16-year-old Ahmad Qassir, who after bidding his mother farewell, urging her to be courageous, and saying he would explain all one day to his father, brothers and sisters, left his village of Deir Qanon e-Nahir, and after being blessed by a Mullah, stepped into the driving seat of his truck-bomb. For fear of Israeli reprisals on his family and village, his name was not disclosed until later (January 1985) when Israeli occupation forces had withdrawn farther south from the area. Posters suddenly appeared, showing Ahmad's face emerging from the ruins of the shattered Israeli HQ building, proclaiming, 'Ahmad Qassir is a Martyr of Islam'.

Terrorists had now gained the initiative in Lebanon. Western Embassies, foreign military contingents, and Israeli detachments took what defensive measures they could. Twenty-feet high walls of earth, sand and stone surrounded camps and compounds where possible; buildings were protected by outer walls of sandbags; twisting narrow chicanes edged with concrete bollards were constructed at entrances to slow vehicles down; and marksmen were posted to shoot any potential suicide-driver attempting to crash through. Usually an armoured car was positioned to block vehicular approaches, which was only removed when the identity of an in-coming vehicle had been satisfactorily ascertained. What was more disconcerting was that no one knew for sure who, or what, 'Islamic Jihad' was. Suspicions were countered by flat denials. Even today there are varying explanations.

Islamic Jihad Since the beginning of the decade, and even before, the code-name 'Islamic Jihad', or more fully 'al-Jihad al-Islami', or variations of it, meaning 'Islamic Holy War', had been used variously and spasmodically by terrorist groups for operations. It is a well-worn Islamic expression, a pious and historical hope, more than a reality, that Muslims everywhere should unite to fight the enemies of Islam. In 1948, a 'Jihad' failed to materialize against Israel, but the expression had a rousing religious ring about it, and inspired young Islamic militants.

In late 1982 and in 1983, it became more frequently used in Lebanon, especially for major terrorist operations, such as those on 23 October. Initially, it was thought to be a new, powerful Muslim Fundamentalist group; but as its exploits multiplied, and became more widespread, doubts arose whether this was really so; or even if it existed at all; or whether by some agreement it was a code-name used universally by a number of different terrorist groups. False and multiple claims of responsibility for terrorist acts were commonplace and almost compulsive. An air of mystery and uncertainty hung over Islamic Jihad.

The Tragedy of Lebanon

Lebanon is a small Mediterranean multi-racial and multi-religious country, which probably had a population (1975 estimate) of just over 3,000,000 people, of whom some 900,000 were Shiahs, the largest of the several sects. For generations the Shiahs inhabited less fertile areas in southern Lebanon, and being politically docile, were traditionally thought of as the 'poor and dispossessed'. In 1957, Imam Musa Sadr, an Iranian-born senior cleric, and life-long friend of Ayatollah Khomeini, was sent to Lebanon to rouse the Shiahs into political awareness; and in 1967, he formed and led the Higher Shiah Communal Council.

Lebanon had a 'cuckoo-in-the-nest', for in 1970–1, after being violently ejected from Jordan, the several Palestine Liberation Organization (PLO) groups and militias, settled forcibly in Southern Lebanon, adjacent to Israel, in Shiah territory, and also in West Beirut, the Muslim part of the Lebanese capital. Weak Lebanese governments and the tiny Lebanese army were unable either to prevent the Palestinians moving in, or to control them when they arrived.

During 1975–6 a bitter civil war raged in Lebanon over sectarian control of government. This devolved into a turmoil of conflicting armed militias struggling for domination, territory or survival. Syrian troops entered the fray, initially to save Christian militias from annihilation, but remained in occupation of northern and eastern parts of the country; Palestinians dominating the south.

Amal During this war Imam Musa Sadr formed a political organization called Amal (Hope), and a militia, the latter taking part in the fighting, giving the Shiahs' self-esteem a boost for the first time. Amal was trained by the PLO, but had an uneasy relationship with its factions due to their overbearing attitude. In August 1978, Imam Musa Sadr disappeared while on a visit to Libya, and has not been seen, or heard of, since. In April 1980, the Amal Congress appointed Nabih Berri, a lawyer, to be its Secretary-General, and he worked to expand Amal, develop its political influence, and build up its militia. An Amal delegation visited Ayatollah Khomeini in Tehran in October 1981, gaining his approbation.

The Israeli Invasion In apparent response to the attempted assassination of their Ambassador in London by Abu Nidal's Fatah-RC, the Israelis launched another military invasion of southern Lebanon (the previous one had been in 1978) on 6 June 1982. This was highly probable anyway since the area was then a hot-bed of PLO activities, and a base for raids into Israel. Eventually, with the aid of Christian militias, the Israelis took West Beirut after a 73-day siege, and ejected PLO militias from the country. Only a partial Israeli withdrawal followed. The South was to remain occupied for the foreseeable future in order to create a permanent security zone for Israel's northern border.

At first the Shiahs had welcomed the invading Israelis, looking on them as deliverers who were removing the oppressive PLO presence, and helped them; but as soon as Israelis collaborated with Christian sects, they turned against them; as did all Muslims in southern Lebanon. Hussein Musavi, a former teacher, now commander of the Amal militia, began guerrilla warfare tactics against the Israeli Army of Occupation, forming and training a number of 'Lebanese Resistance Brigades', which at first used code-names such as 'Amal Jihad' and 'Amal Islami', or variations of them, to claim responsibility for terrorist exploits; but they soon adopted the name 'Islamic Jihad'.

The Shiahs and Resistance There are about 100 million Muslims in the Middle East (estimates vary). About 80 per cent of these are Sunnis, who are generally 'conservative and conventional'; the remainder are Shiahs, or Shiites (Followers of Ali, one of the first Imams), who tend to be 'protesters'. Today, Iran is the only Muslim country with both a Shiah majority and a Shiah government. In 1979, the Shah was overthrown and an Islamic Republic was proclaimed by Ayatollah Khomeini, meaning in fact a 'Shiah' Republic. Khomeini wanted to spread his Shiah persuasion and domination westwards across the Persian Gulf by arousing docile Shiah minorities in Arab Gulf States into seizing power in his name. This surge of militant religious power, usually referred to as 'Islamic Fundamentalism', was a considerable worry to several Muslim states, the fear being that it might inflame their own Shiah minorities.

Martyrdom is highly regarded and respected in Shiah circles. They encourage a disregard for personal safety when fighting for Islamic causes, and Shiahs have developed a particular propensity for it. They also have a taste for flagellation, and tendencies towards mysticism. During the Iran-Iraq War which began in September 1980, tens of thousands of fanatical Shiah Revolutionary Guards and teenagers of the Baseej charged forward time and time again in 'human waves' against strong, sophisticated Iraqi defences. The loss of life was enormous. Musavi harnessed this martyrdom trait, and introduced a *kamikaze* element into his anti-Israeli guerrilla tactics. Most probably it was he who came up with the idea of the suicide-driver and his truck-bomb. In February 1983 he boasted that his Shiah Amal militia had '48 suicide-drivers ready to attack Israeli troops in Lebanon'. In co-operation with Sheikh Mohammed Hassan Fadlallah, a senior Lebanese cleric, Musavi selected and conditioned young Shiahs for suicide-missions.

Not all Shiah attacks in Lebanon against Israeli forces were suicidal. There were dozens of conventional guerrilla and terrorist exploits, such as car-bombs, explosions and ambushes. Also, would-be suicide-drivers did not always carry their missions through to martyrdom; just before Christmas 1983 a truck-bomb was being driven slowly on a suicide-mission near the town of Nasra. As it neared the French

MNF position, the driver jumped out and ran away, leaving his vehicle to roll slowly forward to explode against the compound wall, killing eight French soldiers and wounding seventeen more.

The Hezbollah

When the Israelis invaded southern Lebanon, Ayatollah Khomeini sent 400 of his Revolutionary Guards to Lebanon to join in the Muslim fight against them. The Syrians would not let them go to the forward battle areas, but confined them to Baalbek, in the eastern Beka'a Valley. Sheikh Fadlallah rushed forward to meet them, and in particular to greet the small detachment of Iranian Hezbollah that arrived with them.

The Iranian Hezbollah, meaning Party of God, had sprung into existence as one of the street militias in Tehran that contributed to the downfall of the Shah; and once the Islamic Regime was established they helped it to crush internal enemies. Under the leadership of Hojatolislam Hadi Ghafari, the Hezbollah rose in strength to about 20,000; it had secret links with the ruling Islamic Republican Party (IRP), and played a large part in bringing down Bani-Sadr, the first Islamic President of Iran. Since then, at a much reduced strength, it had become a watch-dog for the IRP.

Sheikh Fadlallah and Sheikh Regeb Ghard (another senior Lebanese Shiah cleric) liaised with the newly arrived Iranian Hezbollah detachment, and set up a comprehensive Islamic-military-political-intelligence structure, as an umbrella organization to draw in guerrilla and terrorist groups. This organization was known simply as the 'Hezbollah', and groups under its influence retained their own titles and entity, and so were able to deny allegations that they were part of it. Money, arms and other support came from Tehran. Khomeini smiled on this new 'Hezbollah' and gave it directives.

The Hezbollah began a campaign of guerrilla warfare and terrorism against the Israeli Army of Occupation and the MNF detachments that had arrived in a peace-keeping role. The Shiah willingness to die in battle quickly made it a greatly feared force.

The Iranian Deputy Foreign Minister, Hussein Sheikholislam, visited Baalbek in January 1984, and congratulated the Hezbollah on its suicide-missions. Strictly speaking all the Islamic Jihad exploits in 1983 had been carried out by Musavi's Amal Lebanese Resistance Brigades, but Musavi was now co-operating with Sheikh Fadlallah, who had become the 'Spiritual Guide' of the Hezbollah.

When Nabih Berri, the Amal leader, joined the Lebanese Coalition Government of Reconstruction in April 1984, Hussein Musavi deserted him and took his Lebanese Resistance Brigades with him; re-naming them 'Islamic Amal', he joined up with Sheikh Fadlallah's Hezbollah in the Beka'a Valley.

As Hezbollah tentacles spread out in southern Lebanon, money was received from Tehran and used for Iranian propaganda amongst Lebanese Shiahs. Posters and pictures of Khomeini were put up; demonstrations were held and political education and welfare work undertaken among the poorer Shiahs, as well as those who had gravitated into the slums of West Beirut, many of whom, owing to circumstances of the war, were in dire straits. Suitable young Shiahs were recruited, trained and indoctrinated ready to take part in the 'armed struggle'. Suspicions were growing in Western minds that the Hezbollah was the basic terrorist organization responsible for the violence, and that Islamic Jihad was just a code-word; but Sheikh Fadlallah cheerfully and flatly denied there was any connection, insisting that his Hezbollah was just a political organization sympathetic to Iranian aims.

The Dawa Iraq, still at war with Iran, also has a large Shiah population (six millions of some fourteen millions), but under a secular Baathist (Arab Socialist) government. Khomeini had expected Iraqi Shiahs, especially as most lived in the eastern provinces adjacent to Iran, to rise against the Baghdad government in his support, but this did not happen, nor did Shiah minorities in other Arab Gulf States turn against their Sunni rulers on behalf of Khomeini.

In the 1960s in Iraq an underground Shiah organization, Hizb al-Daawa al-Islami (the Islamic Call), usually known as 'Dawa', based on the Shiah Holy City of Nejaf, had mounted demonstrations against the government, carried out assassinations, and committed acts of terrorism and sabotage. Many Dawa members were imprisoned, and some executed, by Baath governments. When in exile in Nejaf (1964–78) Khomeini made contact with, and encouraged, Dawa, hoping eventually to use it in furtherance of his long-term plan for his Grand Shiah Revolution. After the Iran-Iraq War began, Khomeini organized the anti-Baathist 'Supreme Council of the Islamic Revolution for Iraq' (SCIRI), scooping together several dissident Iraqi groups, including Dawa, under the leadership of Hojatolislam Mohammed Bakr Hakim, a senior Iraqi cleric.

Dawa elements joined Sheikh Fadlallah's Hezbollah in the Beka'a Valley, and then began to operate in Kuwait, Khomeini's next expansionist target. On 12 December 1983, in Kuwait City, a truck-bomb was driven through the gates of the American Embassy and exploded in the forecourt killing five people. Of the two men in the truck, one was blown to pieces, being later identified as a Dawa member by a thumb whose print was matched in Iraqi Security Forces records. His companion was wounded and arrested. American television had reported the previous August that U.S. Intellgence had foiled an attack on its Kuwaiti Embassy and security was being tightened; if so, they had not done it very effectively.

At about this same time there were five other car-bomb explosions detonated by remote-control elsewhere in Kuwait City; against the French Embassy and other buildings, injuring another 48 people. Responsibility for all the incidents was claimed by Islamic Jihad. A week later ten terrorists, all Dawa members, were arrested in Kuwait; their interrogation led quickly to others. Eventually seventeen Dawa terrorists were tried and convicted, some being sentenced to death, but none were executed. These prisoners became known as the 'Kuwait-17'; and terrorists have repeatedly demanded their release ever since.

Blunder at Bir al-Abed Meanwhile, the American CIA was rapidly coming to the conclusion that the Hezbollah and Islamic Jihad, if not separate groups, were at least working together; that both Iran and Syria were helping them; and that both were under Khomeini's influence. President Reagan had stated that 'in 1983 alone, the CIA either confirmed, or found strong evidence of, Iranian involvement in 57 terrorist attacks'.

The CIA identified Sheikh Fadlallah as the leader of the Hezbollah. They went on the offensive and on 8 March 1984 a car-bomb exploded outside his house at Bir al-Abed, in Southern Beirut. The blast killed 80 people and injured more than 200; the Sheikh had been away at the time and so escaped death. As Minister of Justice in the Lebanese coalition government, Nabih Berri, now estranged from his former military commander, Hussein Musavi, ordered an inquiry, which was inconclusive in its findings although the Iranian Embassy in Beirut was later closed down by the Government. The culprits were most probably Lebanese intelligence agents, hired by the CIA; a later American excuse was that the agents had acted in a free-lance manner without formal permission. Whatever the exact truth, allegations of CIA implication in the Bir al-Abed incident, simply made the fanatical Hezbollah elements more determined to strike back at the 'Great Satan' (America).

Previously, in 1983, the Americans had refused to train Lebanese Government counter-terrorist teams, because such expertise might be used against themselves. The feeling was that the Lebanese regime would not be sufficiently strong to control them. President Reagan had approved certain covert operations against terrorist groups striking against American interests, and the small anti-terrorist unit formed for this purpose was hastily disbanded after the Bir al-Abed exploit.

The following day (9th) a suicide-girl, Sanna Mheidli, drove her car-bomb into an Israeli military convoy near the town of Khiam, close to the Israeli border. Islamic Jihad claimed she killed, not only herself, but also nine Israeli soldiers and injured eleven other people; they said this exploit was in retaliation for the 'Bir al-Abed Massacre'. However, the Israelis stated that apart from the death of the suicide-driver, only two other people were injured, and that there were no Israeli military casualties at all. At first Islamic Jihad communiqués had been reasonably accurate, but they soon began to exaggerate, and then to fictionalize.

The Hezbollah now became bolder and began to operate abroad. On 12 April, an explosion occurred at the Biscano Restaurant, near the US Air Base at Torrejon, in Spain, killing eighteen people, and injuring 83, the casualties being mainly US Servicemen. Responsibility was claimed by Islamic Jihad, which stated that this also was in retaliation for the 'massacre' at Bir al-Abed. A Spanish terrorist group also claimed it, but the hall-marks were those of Hezbollah. A Hezbollah failure occurred in Rome, when on 27 November, it was announced that Security Forces had foiled an attempt to bomb the American Embassy in that city, and that seven people had been arrested in this connection.

Multi-National Withdrawal In February 1984, the US Marine detachment pulled out from the MNF in Lebanon, followed at intervals by the Italian, French and British contingents. The human cost of maintaining a peace-keeping force in that country had been too high. The Hezbollah had driven the MNF out of Lebanon. Terrorism had triumphed.

American diplomats left Muslim West Beirut for safety, moving into an annex building in Christian East Beirut, which was protected against terrorist attack in the usual way. On 20 September, a suicide-driver, drove his truck-bomb at speed through the winding chicane, even though security guards were firing at him, to reach the six-storey building, where it exploded, killing 23 people and injuring 21 others. Both the American Ambassador, and the British Ambassador, who happened to be visiting him, were slightly hurt. There appeared to be no escape from Hezbollah.

Target Kuwait Sometime in mid-1984, Ayatollah Khomeini gave instructions that the Hezbollah leadership in Lebanon was to take control of all Dawa's activities; that the two groups must work together closely; and that Dawa should now concentrate fully upon Kuwait. There had been some friction between Sheikh

Fadlallah and the independently minded Dawa, and also with Musavi and his Islamic Amal group.

The empty Kuwaiti Embassy in Beirut was bombed, and in December 1984, during the period of the trial of the 'Kuwaiti-17', the twin sons of a Kuwaiti diplomat in Beirut were kidnapped; they were eventually released on condition that the name 'Dawa' was not mentioned at all during the trial.

On 4 December (1984), four Dawa members skyjacked a Kuwaiti airliner, just after take-off from Dubai, bound for Pakistan, forcing the pilot to fly the plane to Tehran Airport. Two American passengers were killed during the takeover. The skyjackers demanded the release of the 'Kuwaiti-17'. Their unexpected arrival was not welcomed by the Iranian authorities, and Security Forces surrounded the aircraft. Later a statement was released by the Islamic Republic News Agency (IRNA) that Security Forces had stormed the aircraft, released the passengers and taken the sykjackers into custody. It seems that nothing of the sort happened. This had been a maverick Dawa exploit, carried out without Hezbollah permission. The Khomeini regime had dealt with the matter privately and put on a 'show' for the media.

Dawa continued to concentrate on Kuwait as instructed, and on 1 March 1985 killed an Iraqi diplomat and his young son at his residence in Kuwait City; his wife managed to escape. Responsibility was claimed by Islamic Jihad. In May a suicide-driver rammed the motorcade of Sheikh Jaber al-Ahmad al-Sabah, Ruler of Kuwait, killing three people and injuring twelve, the Sheikh himself being slightly wounded. Again, Islamic Jihad claimed responsibility, demanding the release of the 'Kuwaiti-17'; once again the Ruler refused. In July, two bombs exploded at beach cafes in Kuwait, killing eleven people and injuring 89. Among the dead was the Director of the Criminal Investigation Department. Responsibility was claimed by the Arab Revolutionary Brigades Organization, a new code-name for the Hezbollah; and again the release of the 'Kuwaiti-17' was demanded. Eventually, four people were brought to trial for this exploit, of whom two were sentenced to death.

The Year of the Suicide-Driver By June 1985, Israeli occupation troops were withdrawing further southwards in Lebanon, intending to retire behind a narrow 'security zone', just north of the northern Israeli border, garrisoned by the 'South Lebanon Army' (SLA), consisting mostly of Lebanese Christian mercenaries in Israeli pay. Syrian troops hesitated to move any further southwards in case it provoked the Israelis into military action against them, and so a power vacuum appeared into which Hezabollah activists moved on the heels of the departing Israelis, politicizing the population, and attacking SLA outposts and vehicles.

Even though car-bomb explosions in Lebanon were almost uncountable, particularly in Beirut, 1985 was the worst year since the Embassy attacks of 1983, and it was also notable as the year in which the 'Syrian Socialist Party' (SSNP) became a 'front' organization for the Hezbollah.

After Hezabollah exploits the SSNP would produce communiqués, together with photographs and video-tapes taken of the suicide-drivers before they died, and pass them to the media. The SSNP based itself on the cross-roads town of Chtaura, which was also the HQ of Syrian troops in Lebanon, on the western edge of the Beka'a Valley. It was frequently the target of Israeli attacks and reports from the SSNP and the Israelis often contradicted each other. Later, as Syrian relations with the Iranians became less cordial, the SSNP lost its effectiveness.

Two suicide-driver incidents occurred on 9 July, both against SLA posts in the security zone. In one, a 28-year-old woman, Iptisam Harb, drove a car-bomb at an Israeli position near the village of Ras al-Bayada, in the eastern sector, the SSNP claiming she killed herself and seven Israelis. The other was near Hasbaya in the western sector, when 20-year-old Khalid Azrak, was stopped at a SLA check-point, and ordered to get out of his car to have his identity documents inspected. He jumped back in again quickly, and drove the car-bomb at the post, killing, according to the SSNP, nine people. The Israelis said only the suicide-driver died.

A week later an ambulance loaded with explosives, drove into an Israeli check-point near Tibnin killing nine people. In another incident, 22-year-old Ali Ghazi Taleb drove his car-bomb into an Israeli post near the town of Arnoun (31 July), killing one Israeli and himself, and injuring 20 others. After this exploit, the SSNP produced a video-tape, shown on Lebanese television, of Taleb reading farewell messages to his family. In the background was a photograph of 'Martyr Sanna Mheidli' from whom, he said, he had drawn his inspiration.

It was not absolutely necessary to have a vehicle-bomb to become a martyr. Jamil Sati filled the saddle-bags of his donkey with explosives (6 August) and led the animal to an Israeli check-point near Hasbaya, where both man and donkey were blown to pieces. Only one Israeli was wounded. Responsibility was claimed by the Lebanese National Resistance Front, whose HQ was at Chtaura. It is doubtful if this was a Hezbollah act; it is more likely that it was a copy-cat operation by someone who wanted to become a martyr, which indicates the immense fascination suicide operations had for a Shiah.

More followed in regular sequence; among them eighteen-year old Mariam Kheireddine who drove her car-bomb into an SLA post at dawn on 11 September, killing herself, but only wounding two SLA militiamen. She had not done her homework very well, as by this time Israelis and the SLA were taking precautions against potential suicide-drivers, and no longer 'stood to' at dawn in the conventional military manner, but waited for a couple of hours or so of daylight and observation before re-occupying the post for the day. The SSNP claimed she killed two Israeli officers and ten SLA militiamen; but by this time SSNP claims lacked credence.

Throughout 1986 and 1987 terrorism in Lebanon continued at a high level, and included a number of suicidal exploits. In July 1986 a female car bomber was killed near Jessine, where Hezbollah groups were trying to force a corridor through the Israeli security zone to reach the Israeli frontier proper; elsewhere the Syrians had begun to tighten up their containment of the Hezbollah in the Beka'a Valley.

In the previous July, 1985, George Schultz, US Secretary of State, had said that '60 terrorist raids had been foiled in the last nine months', which gives an idea both of the volume of terrorism, and the rate of terrorist failure. Schultz added, 'Lebanon is a Republic of nihilism where terrorists are given sanctuary'. His statement gives an indication of the effect of counter-terrorist measures, on which far less emphasis was placed by the media.

It was beginning at last to dawn on foreign intelligence agencies that the basic master organization was Hezbollah, and that Islamic Jihad was just a code-name for operations, or perhaps a section of it. One report (The Times, London, 19 May 1985) stated that Ayatollah Khomeini had both knowledge of, and influence over, the Hezbollah, and moreover had given his blessing to its campaign of terrorism, especially Fundamentalist Terrorism. That month Khomeini decreed that the Hezbollah was to consist of 'Units of a few groups of 10-20 people now serving in Lebanon.' Any lingering doubts about the links were soon to be dispelled.

Flight 847 On 14 June 1985, a TWA Boeing 727 left Athens for Rome, with a crew of eight and 145 passengers aboard, mainly Americans. Once airborne the aircraft was taken over by two Hezbollah gunmen, who forced the pilot to fly the aircraft to Beirut. The skyjackers seemed to have been expecting to be met by Amal militiamen, but were disappointed, as none were there. Nonplussed, they released nineteen hostages, mainly women and children, forced the airport authorities to refuel the aircraft, and then, led by Fawaz Younis (code-named Nazar), six Hezbollah terrorists went aboard. The aircraft was then flown to Algiers, where another 21 hostages were released. The skyjackers issued a demand that the Israelis release '766' Muslim prisoners held by them, having moved them from Lebanon to Israel when the Israeli Army of Occupation withdrew southwards. In default the hostages would be killed one by one.

The next day (15th) the TWA aircraft flew back to Beirut, where this time Nabih Berri and his Amal miltiamen were waiting. Berri was hesitant about co-operating with the Hezbollah, as relations between the two organizations had been very cold since the defection of Hussein Musavi. At this stage Beirut Airport was completely encircled by several hostile militias, and the Hezbollah did not have any influence, or leverage, with any of them, and so had no direct access to the airport by land. Amal militiamen controlled a large sector of the airport's southern perimeter. Now, of necessity, the Hezbollah had to persuade Amal to co-operate. To prove their 'seriousness', the skyjackers killed a passenger, an American Serviceman, Robert Stetham, and threw his body out on to the tarmac. Berri then agreed to take charge of negotiations, and four of his Amal militiamen went aboard the aircraft.

The aircraft then returned to Algiers where a number of crew and passengers were released in exchange for the freedom of a Hezbollah accomplice who had been arrested in Athens. On the 16th, the aircraft returned to Beirut for the third time, with 44 hostages on board (three crew and 41 passengers), who were taken from it by Amal militiamen. Four of the captives, being US Servicemen, were taken by the Hezbollah presumably into the Beka'a Valley, the remainder being hidden by Amal in houses in the southern suburbs of Beirut. On the 17th, a sick hostage was released, and on the 18th, three more.

Nabih Berri conducted behind-the-scenes negotiations on behalf of the Hezbollah, with Sheikh Fadlallah, the Iranian Ambassador to Lebanon, Speaker Rafsanjani of the Iranian Majlis (Parliament), Lebanese Ministers and Syrian and Israeli officials. Berri repeatedly said he supported the aims of the Hezbollah, but disagreed with their methods. The aircraft remained on the apron, occupied by Fawaz Younis and his men, and the Amal militiamen, who fended off, and played up to international media representatives. On the 21st, five hostages appeared at a Hezbollah press conference, held somewhere in southern Beirut, the victims saying they were being adequately treated; but already there had been other inpromptu media interviews. On the 22nd, Berri warned the Americans against sabre-rattling; and on the 26th, another sick hostage was released.

Under American pressure the Israelis released 31 Shiah prisoners, insisting this gesture was not skyjack-related. On the 25th, Speaker Rafsanjani, probably the most powerful man in Iran after Khomeini, openly condemned the skyjacking, saying that if he had known about it, he would have tried to prevent it. This was another indication the Hezbollah took its orders, and money, direct from Khomeini, thus by-passing the Iranian Majlis.

Berri continued to try to persuade the Americans to promise not to take reprisals on Lebanese territory, but was unsuccessful until the 24th, when his negotiations were completed. Hostages held by Amal were gathered together in a schoolroom near the airport, to await the arrival of the four held by the Hezbollah; all were then taken by road to Damascus on the 30th, and then flown to Frankfurt.

Reluctantly, the Israelis agreed to release '435 Lebanese and Palestinian' prisoners in four batches, the last of which was freed on 10 September. Already, the Israelis had exchanged 1,150 prisoners, including some convicted for serious terrorist offences, in return for three captured Israeli soldiers. One of the released terrorists had been Kojo Okomato, the single surviving Japanese Red Army member who had conducted the 'Lod Massacre' (May 1972) in which 25 people were killed and 72 injured.

Millions of people watched this 17-day terrorist saga unfold on their television screens with spell-bound suspense, thus giving the terrorists the one thing they desired – publicity. The Israelis seemed to have lost, and although they would perhaps have eventually released most of their prisoners in due course, they were forced to do so prematurely under embarrassing circumstances that smacked loudly of a political trade-off.

Certain sections of the Western media came in for criticism for having entered into a 'symbiotic relationship' with Amal militiamen (exchanging access to hostages for publicity), failing to ask pertinent questions, putting out un-edited material, and for bribery to obtain access to individuals. Terrorism had again triumphed, and the Hezbollah was shown up in all its starkness as a terrorist organization, whose strings were being pulled by Ayatollah Khomeini in Tehran. The code-name 'Islamic Jihad' was used less frequently after this TWA skyjack.

Operation 'Golden Rod' In the aftermath, the US Administration expressed its displeasure with the French for not arresting Imad Mughniyah, a Hezbollah suspect involved in the TWA skyjack, after being informed by the CIA of his presence in France. The Lebanese Government announced its intention to prosecute Fawaz Younis, Ali Atwi, Ahmad Gharibeh, Mohammed Ali Hamadei, and others, believed to be principals in the TWA skyjack, but as all were still at large, this declaration was symbolic and ineffectual.

Far more effective was American action on 18 September, when in furtherance of President Reagan's 'They can run but they can't hide' policy, Fawaz Younis, was snatched in Operation 'Golden Rod', by CIA agents from a rented yacht sailing off Cyprus, transferred to a US warship, and flown to the USA to stand trial for the murder of the US serviceman on the TWA aircraft.

Kuwaiti Skyjack: 1988 The cycle repeated itself in 1988 with a Hezbollah-organized skyjack exploit to try to obtain the release of the 'Kuwaiti-17'; this was probably largely organized and executed by the same personnel involved the TWA skyjack of 1985, who had taken to heart many of the lessons extracted from that rather jumbled operation. A Kuwait Airlines 747 Jet with 122 people on board, flying from Bangkok to Kuwait, was skyjacked on 5 April, by a Hezbollah team of probably seven men, who had boarded the plane at Bangkok, armed with a couple of pistols and a grenade. This was the first team, whose task was to seize the aircraft, which was diverted to Mashad, in north-east Iran, where it stood for three days. This time it was expected by the authorities, and under a guise of besieging the aircraft with Security Forces, the second team, probably led by Imad Mughniyah, a veteran of the TWA skyjack of 1985, took over from the original one. This team was professional in its attitude, trained and geared for this exploit, and took aboard with it automatic weapons, explosives, grenades and communication equipment. The new team, of eight men, were all hooded right from the beginning, spoke little and never mentioned names when they talked to one another. The Club Class accommodation became their operations centre; the passengers were pushed back into the Cabin Class section of the aircraft and saw only those detailed to guard them, knowing nothing of what was happening. The majority of the passengers were Kuwaitis, three being distant relatives of Sheikh Jaber al-Ahmad al-Sabah, Ruler of Kuwait, who were kept in uncomfortable, cramped conditions with their wrists bound.

It seems that the plan was to be a repeat of the 1985 exploit: landing the Jumbo Jet at Beirut Airport and taking the Kuwaiti hostages from the plane into captivity in either the southern suburbs or the Beka'a Valley, but Berri's Amal militiamen had been losing out in the fighting for territory around the airport.

On the 9th, the Jumbo Jet left Mashad heading for Beirut, where permission to land was refused; Syrian troops blocked the runways with vehicles, and threatened to shoot the aircraft down if it tried to land. This was a shock to the skyjackers, who had not realized that relations between Syria and Iran over hostage issues had deteriorated so badly. The aircraft circled Beirut Airport for some time, threatening a suicidal crash-landing. Then, short of fuel, they asked for permission to land at nearby Damascus, and this was firmly refused; another shock for the Hezbollah team aboard. At the last moment Cypriot authorities, on humanitarian grounds, said that the Jumbo Jet could land at Larnaca Airport, which it did, its fuel all but exhausted.

Isolated by a Security Forces cordon, the aircraft stayed in Cyprus for six days, during which negotiations took place. During this period two hostages, both Kuwaiti men (and Sunnis incidentally) were shot dead on separate days and their bodies were pushed out on to the apron; a total of twelve hostages, mainly non-Kuwaitis, were released. Terrorist threats to kill more hostages, forced the Larnaca Airport authorities to refuel the aircraft, and allow it to fly to Algiers on the 13th.

Throughout, the Ruler of Kuwait steadfastly refused to accede to demands to release the 'Kuwaiti-17'. The skyjackers remained calm and confident and at times there were pauses in negotiations, seemingly as if the terrorists were waiting for further instructions from their superiors. Dramatics were indulged in, and for example, the skyjackers at one point donned 'Martyrs' Shrouds, and threatened to blow up the aircraft, their hostages and themselves, but it did not come to that.

Suddenly on the 20th, it was all over. Before dawn the team of skyjackers quietly left the aircraft, and were quickly flown out of Algeria; it is thought first to Libya, and then back to Lebanon. The 31 remaining hostages were freed and their 16-day ordeal was over, being the longest-running skyjack hostage situation so far anywhere in the world. Western intelligence agencies claimed they knew exactly who the skyjackers were, having obtained details by means of sophisticated listening and other devices, but refused to divulge their identities, saying that this would compromise their methods and equipment used.

Two factors brought this exploit to an abrupt end. The first was the determination of the Ruler of Kuwait, and the fact there was no sign of his ever changing his mind; the second was the onset of Ramadan, the month in which Muslims fast, taking neither food nor drink during daylight hours, which would have sapped their determination, both pyschologically and physically. Despite their dedication, training, expertise and planning, their fortitude was beginning to crack.

The British and American Governments were angry because the skyjackers had been allowed to escape, condemning both Iran (not being absolutely certain at the time of its full involvement) and Cyprus for refuelling the aircraft, and allowing it to fly off again; and Algeria for agreeing to spirit the skyjackers away. Certainly, Iran, Libya, Algeria and the PLO had all negotiated, colluded and co-operated with the terrorists. The Hezbollah had avoided defeat, but had not achieved victory, as the 'Kuwaiti-17' still remained in prison in Kuwait. America and Britain saw it as a defeat in the fight against terrorism, the terrorists having escaped justice.

Lebanese Revolutionary Armed Faction Another Lebanese-based, Hezbollah-related terrorist group was the Lebanese Revolutionary Armed Faction (FARL). Formed in 1980, by Georges Ibrahim Abdullah, a Lebanese Maronite Christian, who was vaguely anti-Imperialist, its early targets were mainly Jewish and American. FARL was always small, seldom having more than 20 activists, who were Adbullah, his four brothers (Maurice, Robert, Emile and Joseph), and members of his extended family. Abdullah had trained with the Italian Red Brigades in 1979, and so became one of the 'international terrorist fraternity', making good contacts with other terrorist groups.

FARL's major exploits were in France, and included the assassination of Colonel Charles Ray, US Deputy Defence Attaché, who was shot in Paris in January 1982. In April it killed Yacov Barsimantov, a senior Israeli diplomat, in the same manner. In August FARL claimed responsibility for a large bomb detected outside the house of an American diplomat in Paris which exploded as it was being dismantled, killing one policeman and fatally wounding another. Other FARL exploits followed, mainly in and around Paris; then suddenly, on 25 October 1982, posing as an Algerian, Abdullah walked into a police station in Lyons, seeking protection 'against the Israeli Mossad', which he claimed was constantly following him. In fact it was not the Mossad, but the French internal secret service, the Direction de la Surveillance du Territoire (DST). Inquires revealed him to be the leader of FARL; his apartment was searched, and a cache of arms and false identity papers was discovered. Abdullah was eventually sentenced to four years' imprisonment for illegal possesssion of these items.

In March 1985 a Frenchman, Gilles Payrolles, was seized as a hostage in Lebanon and the demand was made that Abdullah be freed from prison, in exchange for the hostage's freedom. In the meantime, however, a pistol found in Abdullah's apartment had been identified as the weapon that killed Ray and Barsimantov, and this caused the French to renege on a secret exchange agreement, under which the Frenchman had already been released.

In the interim, attacks resumed in France with a spate of exploits aimed chiefly against Jewish and American targets; the object being to obtain the release of not only Abdullah, but also an Armenian terrorist (Varadjian Dardidjian) and a Palestinian (Anis Nacache). This indicated a degree of international solidarity. Responsibility for these acts was claimed by the Comité de Solidarité avec les prisonniers Politiques arabs et du Proche-Orient (CSPPA), |Committee for Solidarity with Middle Eastern and Arab Political Prisoners| – which in fact was FARL. One of these incidents was a bomb explosion on the Paris Metro (underground railway system) on 6 September 1986; another was an explosion a week later at a police building annex. There were others, and in the spate of bombing in September that year, eleven people were killed and more than 200 injured; responsibility for all being claimed by the CSPPA.

Georges Ibrahim Abdullah, leader of FARL, was brought to trial on the double murder charge in Paris, in February 1987, being the first to be held under new legislation which replaced a jury of laymen by a board of seven professional magistrates. Several of Abdullah's brothers appeared in France. In March, a bomb exploded in a Champs Elysée shopping area, killing two people and injuring 20, responsibility being claimed by the CSPPA. In Lebanon FARL was liaising with the Hezbollah, and it was common knowledge that the French authorities wanted the Court to award a lenient sentence to Abdullah, so that he could be exchanged for a French hostage held in Lebanon; and it was to general surprise that he was sentenced to life imprisonment in July.

The Hostage Crisis

As the Iran-Iraq War stalemated on land, Ayatollah Khomeini sought other means of reaching out to strike at the Great Satan, and his other enemies overseas. The seizure of the American Embassy in Tehran by Revolutionary students in November 1979 and the holding of American hostages for 444 days amidst the continuing blaze of publicity that ensured; American helplessness and the high Western regard for the sanctity of human life, had made a deep impression on many in the Middle East, and especially on Khomeini. The taking and holding of hostages on an internecine basis had long been common practice in Lebanon, and many Lebanese sects and factions with sizeable militias, had their own 'prisons' for this purpose; hostages being regarded as an essential form of insurance none could afford to be without. Conditions in these 'prisons' varied, but most were primitive, and hostages suffered hardship and deprivation, being usually kept in darkness, sometimes chained and bound, in tiny rooms, often with taped music continually playing to prevent the victim identifying sounds that might later help to locate the site.

Khomeini began to use the Hezbollah for this purpose, and one of the first Americans to be kidnapped, on 16 March 1984, was William Buckley, CIA Station Chief at the American Embassy in Beirut. Responsibility was claimed by Islamic Jihad, which stated in October that it had 'executed' him; no positive information about him has been forthcoming since then. By 1985, the Hezbollah was holding eleven American and French hostages, and a few others of different nationalities. By mid-1987, the number had risen and included nine Americans, six French, and three British. During this period five hostages had been killed, or presumed killed (one American, one Russian and three British) while one American had 'escaped'. A few had been released, reputedly for huge ransoms, although such details were consistently denied by all parties to such deals.

Soviet Deference The first kidnapping of east European personnel occurred on 30 September 1985, when four Russians were seized in Beirut by the Islamic Liberation Organization, an occasional code-name for the Hezbollah which automatically denied any implication in the exploit. Presumably the object had been to persuade the Russians to put pressure on Syria to step in and end the fighting between rival militias in Tripoli (Lebanon). The body of one of the Russians was discovered a few days later on some waste ground in Beirut. More than 30 Soviet diplomats and 120 other Russian personnel, including media staff, were immediately evacuated to Damascus; meanwhile, according to PLO sources, a male relative of Sheikh Fadlallah was kidnapped and killed, his private parts, in a cellophane bag with a medical explanatory note, were then sent to the Sheikh. The three other detained Russians were quickly released, and no Russians have since been abducted in Lebanon.

Terry Waite Considerable publicity was given to Terry Waite, the Archbishop of Canterbury's special envoy, who shuttled to and from Lebanon during 1985, being responsible it is claimed for the release of at least three American hostages. On 10 January 1987 Waite was himself kidnapped in Beirut, after leaving the protection of the Druse leader, Walid Jumblatt. It was presumed to be the work of Hezbollah, which had indirectly alleged that he was an American spy. It seems that American sources were funding Waite, and that when captured he had a CIA 'bug' in his hair.

Hostages were held mainly in the Shiah slums of West Beirut, which had devolved into a state of anarchy, with armed militias struggling among themselves for territory and influence, including that of the Hezbollah. Syrian troops remained in occupation of northern and eastern parts of Lebanon. Even though the Syrian Intelligence Agency, and its covert operations arm, Saiqa, retained some contact with the Hezbollah, friction had developed between them, especially over the hostage issue.

Syrian troops then suddenly swept into West Beirut on 22 February 1986, overcoming opposition from Shiite and other militias, and in one incident killed 22 Hezbollah personnel in an HQ building, who would neither surrender nor evacuate. The Hezbollah hastily moved its hostages into the slum areas of southern Beirut, which Syrian troops stopped short of entering in case captives were killed. Enjoying the attendant publicity and helplessness of foreign powers, the Hezbollah seemed in no hurry to release its hostages.

The Hamadei Brothers Hezbollah activities in western Europe continued and on 13 January 1987, Mohammed Ali Hamadei, a Shiah Labanese, and a member of Hezbollah, was arrested in Frankfurt, carrying a false passport and three bottles of liquid explosive in his luggage. Hamadei had been deeply involved in the TWA skyjack of 1985, his finger-prints being found on the aircraft; later at an identification parade, a former hostage picked him out as one of the terrorists on the aircraft. The Americans immediately demanded his extradition, but the West German Government chose to put him on trial themselves instead.

A few days later they paid the price when two West Germans, Rudolf Cordes and Alfred Schmidt, were kidnapped in Lebanon by the Hezbollah. Abbas Hamadei (brother of Mohammed), who had become a West German citizen, was then also arrested at Frankfurt Airport (on the 26th), with explosives in his possession. He was charged with involvement in the kidnapping of the two West Germans.

During the lengthy debate as to whether Mohammed Hamadei should be extradited to the USA, or not, an American journalist, Charles Glass, who had a deep knowledge of Lebanese affairs, and in fact had covered the TWA skyjack of 1985, was kidnapped in Lebanon by the Hezbollah on 17 June. Glass managed to 'escape' 62 days later; but as this occurred after the West German decision not to extradite Mohammed Hamadei to the USA had been made, it aroused speculation as to whether his 'escape' had been contrived.

The London Accord   Meanwhile, concern for hostages held in Lebanon increased, and at an EEC summit meeting in London on 12 December 1986, it was agreed that no concessions under duress should be made to terrorists for the release of any hostages. This became known as the London Accord. The first country to breach this Accord was West Germany, which allowed a huge ransom, reputed to be more than $2,000,000, to be paid together with a large quantity of medical supplies, by the firm that employed Alfred Schmidt, who was released on 7 September 1987. Schmidt had been periodically chained up during his captivity. A West German Chancellery Minister, and Member of the Crisis Staff formed for the incident, later admitted in his evidence at the trial of Abbas Hamadei at Düsseldorf, that 'kidnapping' had played a part in preventing Mohammed Hamadei's extradition to the USA. The other West German, Cordes, remained a hostage. The Hezbollah seemed to deliberately select certain hostages employed by large multi-national commercial concerns able, and willing, to pay large ransoms.

In the following month, another hostage, a South Korean diplomat, Do Chae Sung, was kidnapped in Beirut, responsibility being claimed by the Revolutionary Commando Cells, another Hezbollah code-name. Do was quietly released in October 1987, being ransomed for $2,000,000. This left the Hezbollah still holding about 26 hostages. Another West German citizen, Ralph Seray-Scray, was kidnapped in Lebanon on 27 February 1988, by the Holy Warriors of Freedom, a new Hezbollah code-name, in an attempt to obtain the release of both Mohammed Ali Hamadei and Abbas Hamadei. This exploit was organized by Abdul Hadi Hamadei (another brother), described as a 'Security Officer' of Hezbollah.

French Duplicity   Previously, French negotiations with Iranians for the release of French hostages held in Lebanon had been unsuccessful and had lapsed, but when Jacques Chirac's government came into power in March 1986, secret negotiations were resumed. In July 1987, French Security Forces wanted to arrest an Iranian, Vahid Gordji, who was working as an interpreter at the Iranian Embassy in Paris, as he was suspected of being involved in a series of bombings in the city the previous year, in which fourteen people had died. The Iranians refused to surrender him, even through he did not have diplomatic immunity. A metal fence was erected around the Iranian Embassy, and French Security Forces checked all who entered and left the building to prevent Gordji escaping. In riposte, Iranian Security Forces surrounded the French Embassy in Tehran in a like manner, imprisoning the remaining French diplomat in residence, Raul Torri. This tense siege and counter-siege situation dragged on while secret French-Iranian negotiations continued.

Suddenly, in November, two French hostages, Roger Auque and Jean-Louis Normandin, both working for French television, were released; this left three still in captivity in Lebanon. Vahid Gordji, after briefly appearing before a French examining magistrate, was quickly released, the official excuse being that it was 'purely a matter for the French judiciary'. That same day, Torri was released, the exchanges actually taking place at Karachi Airport.

However, it soon became apparent that there were political conditions attached to this exchange, which breached the London Accord. A large ransom was paid by someone in France to the Revolutionary Justice Organization, a Hezbollah code-name. France also agreed to slow down the rate of arms delivery to Iraq, meaning the promised twenty Mirage F-1 aircraft. It was made known that France had already illegally supplied artillery shells to Iran, and it was agreed that France would reduce its naval contribution to the Persian Gulf Western embargo fleet; the aircraft carrier *Clemenceau* was then withdrawn. France was to stop making threats against the Iranian regime, improve its relations with that country, and pay one-third ($333,000,000) as a first instalment repayment on a billion dollar loan contracted by the late Shah. It was thought that another similar instalment was demanded for the other three French hostages, released on 4 May 1988: Marcel Fontaine, a diplomat; Marcel Carton, a diplomatic employee; and Jean-Paul Kaufmann, a journalist.

First West Germany, and now France, had blatantly broke the London Accord to suit their own convenience, and shattered the unity of purpose of the EEC against terrorism. An angry British Prime Minister stated there would be no such negotiations for the three British hostages. Previously, she had been praising French Security Forces for intercepting a ship carrying Libyan arms destined for the Irish Republican Army.

Most foreigners kept away from Beirut, and those whose business or duty compelled them to go there took precautions against being kidnapped, but even so it was dangerous for the unwary. In February 1988, Lieutenant-Colonel W. Higgins, the newly appointed Head of the UN Truce Supervisory Organization (UNTSO) was seized by the Hezbollah. Newly arrived in Lebanon, he had not yet been through the customary counter-terrorist survival course, and had been alone, driving a UN vehicle, when caught. Higgins was listed in the Pentagon Telephone Book (on sale to the public) as being on the staff of the Secretary of Defense. The Hezbollah claimed he was a CIA Agent, and said he would be tried as a spy.

An Arm of the State

The formerly elusive and mysterious 'Islamic Jihad' which had perplexed Western intelligence agencies for so long, had turned out to be but a code-name, at first used frequently by Hezbollah factions. The Hezbollah continually protested that it had nothing to do with terrorism, but was simply a political organization, working for Lebanese Shiah status and welfare. Under the leadership and direction of Sheikhs Fadlallah, Ibrahimal-Amin Sobhi Tofeili, and Hussein Musavi, the Hezbollah developed into a terrorist coalition, directed and funded by Ayatollah Khomeini of Iran. Within it several Shiah groups operated, pooling intelligence and resources, and developing some international terrorist contacts. The Hezbollah also formed its own militia arm in Lebanon, thought to be more than 2,000 strong, which took part in the internecine fighting in and around Beirut, and protected their base and camps in the Beka'a Valley.

The Hezbollah was a blatant example of State Terrorism, operating by proxy in a modern scenario. This was occasionally half admitted: in July 1985, Musavi told the media, 'The Imam (Khomeini) is our Supreme Leader . . . Hezbollah finances come from Tehran.' His comments were endorsed by Sheikh Fadlallah, who added, 'We (Hezbollah and Khomeini) work in the same framework.' Iranian State Terrorism, in the form of the Fundamentalist Hezbollah, is alive and flourishing, living in West and South Beirut, and in the Beka'a Valley in Lebanon, taking its orders from Tehran.

4. The Irish Republican Army

An IRA
propaganda
poster from
1981.
(Henshaw
Collection)

'Violence by Freedom Fighters is the only force likely to affect British Government policy.' –
Acceptance Speech by Gerry Adams, as President of the Provisional Sinn Fein,
Dublin, November 1983

N deeply troubled Northern Ireland (NI) on 1 January 1980, the decade began
with a Roman Catholic (RC) man dying in hospital after being shot at his home in
Belfast by a terrorist; on the 2nd, a former Ulster Defence Regiment (UDR)
member was shot dead outside his house in County (Co) Armagh; on the 3rd, a
Police reservist was killed by a gunman in Co Fermanagh; and on the 4th, a
Catholic man was found beaten to death in Belfast – all for political reasons. The
'Roll of Horror' for that year eventually totalled 75 terrorist-related deaths, and 801
persons injured. 'Republican' terrorist groups were locked in a struggle with British
Security Forces, and also with 'Loyalist' terrorist groups; a situation that had
obtained since 1969. Since 1972, when provincial government was suspended, NI
had been governed directly from Westminster, through a Ministerial Secretary of

State. The British Government was determined to maintain the status quo of 'majority rule'; Republican groups were determined to achieve a 'United Ireland'; and 'Loyalist' organizations were equally determined to prevent that Republican goal being attained.

In 1980, the population of NI was about 1.5 millions of which about one-million were 'Protestants' (or non-Roman Catholics), being mainly 'Loyalists', that is loyal to Ulster's Union with Britain; the remainder being Roman Catholic with Nationalist, often Republican ideals and an emotional desire to unite with the Republic of Ireland (ROI) under a government in Dublin. Although many people still resided in 'mixed' communities, especially in rural areas, sectarian violence had caused a majority to gravitate to cities and towns, which in themselves had traditionally segregated districts, some people being huddled in ghetto-like areas for their own security, as in Belfast or Londonderry ('Derry' to the Republicans). Separate sectarian schools taught different religions, different interpretations of history and politics, and perpetuated prejudices and fears. During their early years children of one community hardly ever mixed with children of the other and so unconsciously absorbed hostile propaganda that each put out against the other.

The Republican Movement

The 1916 Rising The Irish Republican Army (IRA) stems from the 1916 'Easter Rising' in Dublin against British Rule, which was put down with great severity and brutality; and was forged in detention camps in Wales. Reformed in 1919, it began guerrilla warfare against the British military presence in Ireland, a period the Irish call the 'Black-and-Tan War' (from the uniform of the British security personnel brought in to combat the IRA).

In December 1919, Prime Minister Lloyd George legislated for two Irish 'parliaments', one in Dublin, for the RC majority in the south; and one in Belfast, for the Protestant minority in the north. The Anglo-Irish Treaty brought the 'Irish Free State', of '26 counties', into being in December 1921. Protestant leaders in the north had already accepted a Parliament in Belfast, which had opted to be linked with Britain. Three counties were hived off from the traditional Province of Ulster to the new Irish Free State to ensure the remaining six counties produced a Protestant majority in the Belfast provincial government.

Acceptance of the Irish Free State caused a split within the IRA, a hard-line element feeling it should have fought on for a 'United Ireland'. A bitter civil war ensued between the 'Free Staters' and IRA purists, in which the latter were disastrously defeated. The IRA was not able to reform until the late 1920s. Eamon de Valera, a former IRA leader, formed the Fianna Fail (Soldiers of Destiny) Party, which gained a majority in the 1932 election, bringing him to power as Prime Minister, but he did not release his former colleagues, many of whom remained in detention; and indeed in 1936, he proscribed the organization.

The IRA carried out some terrorist activities in England from 1938 to 1941; but, after the Second World War had begun, fearing such activity might provoke the British into a military invasion of Eire [Ireland] (as the Free State had been re-named), de Valera cracked down hard on his old organization.

The IRA launched an abortive campaign in Northern Ireland (1956–62) which failed through lack of popular support; after which it lay low to recuperate, and was caught by surprise in 1969, by spontaneous Civil Rights marches and demonstrations, and the support and enthusiasm they suddenly engendered. Belatedly, the IRA hesitantly moved to turn this Civil Rights campaign into an 'armed struggle' for a United Ireland, and to eject the British military presence from NI once and for all.

The Provisional IRA Almost immediately there were disputes within the IRA over the policy to be adopted, provoked by the seeming indifferent of the IRA GHQ in Dublin, and its reluctance to take aggressive action. A group of activists broke away from the main body, to become known as the 'Provisional IRA' (PIRA), or 'Provos'; while the staid parent body became known as the 'Official IRA', or the 'Old Stickies'. The political wing of the IRA, the Sinn Fein (Ourselves Alone) movement, also divided into the 'Official Sinn Fein' and the 'Provisional Sinn Fein'. There had always been two competing factions within the old IRA, one very left-wing orientated, forever dreaming of a revolution of the 'people' on the Russian 1917 pattern; and the other, more hardline and activist that believed in the 'armed struggle'. During the Spanish Civil War (1936–9) for example, elements of these two IRA factions had fought on opposite sides, and against each other.

In 1969, for a period, both IRA factions operated against the British Security Forces, but at times they clashed over territory and the distribution of weapons. In May 1972, the Official IRA declared a Truce with the British, which still remains in force, and since then this group has remained largely dormant. The strength of PIRA in 1980 meanwhile (RUC estimates) was just over 1,000 regular volunteers, of whom less than half were 'activists'.

Irish National Liberation Army In 1974, exasperated by its inaction, a splinter group broke away from the Official IRA to form the Irish Republican Socialist Party (IRSP), which the following year formed a military wing, the Irish National Liberation Army, (INLA). The parting between the Official IRA and the INLA was not a happy one, and the two factions fought each other: on 6 December 1980, in Dublin, two masked men shot and seriously wounded Harry Flynn, the Chief of Staff of the INLA; they were presumed to be Official IRA members. In 1980, the INLA, which operated from Dublin, had only just over 100 members, but practically all were activists.

The Republican Movement, to use a generic term, is given to splits and therefore the abbreviation 'IRA' is used to cover the entire multitude of political and military groups, the largest among them being the Provisional IRA and its political wing, Sinn Fein.

Organization Due to the 'Heritage of Hate' [1] left behind by the British coupled with the emotive ideal of fighting for a United Ireland, the IRA was seldom short of volunteers, and indeed the basic rank of members was that of 'Volunteer'. Additionally from the late 1960s on another motivating force has been the worst social and economic conditions in the United Kingdom (UK), coupled with Protestant sectarian prejudice against the Catholic population embodied in the provincial government echelons.

Membership of the IRA always had a prestige attraction to young RC men, and despite the necessity for secrecy, most Volunteers liked to be known, and pointed out, as 'one of the boys'. Those joining terrorist organizations mostly mount a tiger, and cannot dismount. In this respect the IRA is different, as under certain

[1] For an account of the IRA in the 1970s, and before, see *Terror in Ireland: The Heritage of Hate*, by Edgar O'Ballance. Columbus Books (UK), 1981

circumstances it allows Volunteers to resign, and occasionally dismisses them; then, all they have to do is to keep their mouths shut. For example, following the structural changes in 1977–8, the IRA had a surplus of manpower, which was disposed of in this way. This method also provides a hidden 'IRA reserve', which can be called upon when required, as well as 'sleepers' and 'moles'.

The old IRA had a military-style organization, modelled on that of its early adversary, the British Army. It adopted a military structure of brigades, battalions and companies; designations such as Chief of Staff, Adjutant-General and Quartermaster; and its disciplinary procedures. A series of set-backs, failures and leakages of information, caused the PIRA to make a radical re-organization in 1977–8, after studying certain international terrorist groups. Large formations were abandoned, and in their place appeared small secret cells, each of half-a-dozen or so Volunteers, called 'Active Service Units' (ASUs), which (in theory) were unknown to one another, with a vertical chain of command. The object was to preserve secrecy, which had been wanting. However, the 'Brigade' formation was retained as a territorial command, named after a locality, being responsible for the ASUs within its area. Some, like the Belfast Brigade had many ASUs, and others like the West Fermanagh Brigade, had only two or three.

The IRA has always been controlled by a small Army Council, of eight or so members, one of whom was the Chief of Staff, being the senior executive officer, and the others were usually Directors of the main branches, such as Intelligence, Operations or Procurement. At times Army Councils have been in conflict with the Sinn Fein Party, its political wing; sometimes both have worked well together. IRA and Sinn Fein leaders often held dual appointments in both organizations, and it is suspected that this practice still continues.

The Provisional Sinn Fein is legal in both parts of Ireland, and indeed holds its Annual Convention (Ard Feis) openly in Dublin. In 1980, Rory O'Brady was President, Gerry Adams was Deputy President, and others on the Council included Martin McGuiness, Ivor Bell and Danny Morrison. In contrast, a dark veil of secrecy clouded the illegal PIRA Army Council, and even the Royal Ulster Constabulary's (RUC) Intelligence Unit was never actually sure who held which appointment. In 1980, it was assumed that Gerry Adams was the PIRA Chief of Staff.

Funding the 'war effort'   IRA funds have always been obtained by the usual illegal means: protection rackets; levies on captive communities; bank, and other, robberies; and extortion. These methods have become open secrets that cause the British Government some concern. In September 1982, the Chief Constable of the RUC established a team (known as 'C-13') to investigate these practices and, in particular, to examine extortion from business and industry, VAT evasion and false claims, plus 'fronts' that collect and 'launder' illegal money. In fact, there was little the authorities could do, owing to local intimidation. At times criminal greed overcame political purity, and not only did factions divide territory between them for extortion purposes, but in some 'mixed' areas Republican and Loyalist para-military groups secretly agreed to do the same.

The PIRA also obtained funds from legal sources in the USA, through such organizations as 'Noraid' (Northern Aid Committee), still run by an IRA veteran, Michael Flannery. Strictly, these American funds were for the welfare of the families of PIRA men killed, in detention, or on the run; but much is misused for purchasing arms and financing PIRA activities.

By the mid-1980s, PIRA was feeling the financial pinch, as since 1981, the British Government had been using both diplomatic pressure, and a publicity campaign in the USA, which had persuaded the American Administration that Noraid was simply an agent for the IRA, and had to be registered under special laws. Irish Republican extremists, who formerly visited America on fund-raising tours, were bannned. A reduced income from Noraid, and a tightening up of security measures in the ROI, where bank and post office robberies had brought the PIRA considerable sums of money for many months, brought both financial problems and subsequent internal argument. The RUC estimated that about £2,000,000 a year was required to fund both Sinn Fein's politcal campaign, and PIRA's terrorist activities and social disbursements.

In 1983, the PIRA had bungled three attempts to raise large sums of money in the ROI from ransom demands. These were the abduction of the Derby Winning race-horse 'Shergar'; Galen Weston, a supermarket chief; and Don Tidy, a supermarket executive. Had they all been successful, the PIRA might have netted about £12,000,000; instead they ended in shoot-outs and capture. Also, in February 1985, Irish Security Forces discovered a large sum of money in an Irish Bank, reputed to be almost £5,000,000, belonging to the PIRA, which the Irish Government sequestered.

The 20-man RUC C-13 anti-corruption team did its best, notching up 117 convictions by the end of 1987; but it was too small to be really effective, as rackets had multiplied, to include not only social clubs, taxi businesses, and levies on other businesses and individuals, but also big-time cattle smuggling across the border into the ROI, and VAT frauds.

John McMichael, Deputy Leader of the Ulster Defence Association (a Protestant para-military group), was killed by a car-bomb on 22 December 1987, in what was thought to be a joint IRA-UDA set-up to get rid of him, as he had been investigating protection rackets run by his own organization. A British television programme had spot-lighted these activities, alleging that opposing terrorist groups were making agreements with one another over territory. The issue caused feuding within the UDA's leadership and early in 1988 the leader, Andy Tyrie, was ousted by the UDA Council which pledged a hard line against racketeering.

Arms Procurement In 1980, the RUC estimated that the IRA had about 5,000 arms of various types (probably five for every Volunteer), including revolvers and pistols (hand-guns in the parlance), rifles, automatic weapons and grenades, obtained illegally from sources in the USA, international terrorist groups, and Libya. The IRA had long had its own ample source of explosives manufactured in garage-workshops, from readily obtainable ingredients, such as bleach, weed-killer, sugar, ammonia, diesel oil, petrol, and agricultural fertilizers. The PIRA was able to home produce bombs and land-mines of gigantic size and energy, the explosive material usually being packed into metal beer kegs or fertilizer sacks; many of which exceeded 800 pounds in weight. The record was one of nearly 3,000 pounds, in 60 fertilizer sacks wired together, discovered in October 1987, in a derelict farm building at Bellaghy, Co Tyrone, and defuzed.

The PIRA has also produced a home-made 'Mark 10 Mortar', carried on a lorry, which formed its base-plate. Owing to its unreliability and inaccuracy, it is often more dangerous to its handlers, and those in the vicinity, than to the target. On one occasion it missed its police station target in Newry, Co Down, injuring 32 civilians instead; but its efficiency has slowly improved. Also, a few PIRA 'bomb-makers' have developed considerable expertise in assembling detonators and devices, including remote-control, radio-detonated, and 'mercury-tilt' switches.

As early as August 1981, the PIRA brought its Soviet RPG-7 (Rocket-Propelled Grenade) into action in Belfast against an Army armoured vehicle, injuring two people; and the following months, an RPG-7 struck an RUC vehicle, killing one policeman and injuring another. These potentially deadly missiles were probably obtained from Libya; they have been used on numerous occasions since, often resulting in fatalities.

The Mark 10 Mortar meanwhile was brought into action for the eighteenth time on 25 February 1985, against the Police Station at Newry, killing nine RUC members (including two policewomen), and injuring 57 others. Nine converted gas-cylinder tubes, wired together, had been used, each containing a 40lb 'bomb', positioned on the back of a lorry and looking like a Soviet 'Stalin Organ' (multiple rocket-launcher). A timing device enabled operators to get clear, and nine bombs were projected in a 'ripple', but only one made a direct hit on the police station; two exploded in the air; two fell in front of the station wrecking a few cars; two exploded harmlessly in a derelict building, and the other two failed to explode at all. The mortar would have taken about an hour to set up, on some nearby wasteland, and the RUC was negligent in not detecting it in time. The PIRA crowed, 'This was a major and well-planned operation, indicating our ability to strike where and when we decide,' but the fact remained that the Mark 10 Mortar was still a crude hit-or-miss weapon, with less than rule-of-thumb accuracy. It has remained a frequently used IRA weapon though, probably due to its propaganda value. In November 1986 it was directed against the joint Army-RUC post at Middletown, Co Armagh, wounding five soldiers; again in April 1987 against Bessebrook Army Base, injuring two soldiers, when seven of its sixteen bombs failed to explode, and all but one of the others were wildly inaccurate.

The INLA continually searched for arms and explosives, obtaining only a few from sympathetic Euro-terrorist groups. However, it did find a source in the USA, and small quantities were forwarded in sea-containers to Rotterdam, and carried in vehicles by car-ferry, usually to Le Havre, and thence again by ferry to Rosslaire, in the Republic.

This route had its hazards, as French police became suspicious. On 28 August 1982, three INLA members: Michael Plunkett, a former General Secretary of the IRSP; Stephen King; and Mary Reid, a former editor of *The Starry Plough*, the IRSP newspaper, were arrested by French police for arms smuggling. The accused insisted that the police had 'planted' arms on them; all charges were eventually dropped, and the police concerned subsequently disciplined. All three were 'wanted' in the ROI, but the French granted them political asylum. In August, the following year, French police discovered arms on the Le Havre ferry, and Michael MacDonald, an INLA member, was convicted. The next INLA misfortune occurred in June 1986, when seven INLA members were arrested in France, after a vehicle containing twelve assault rifles, 22 hand-guns, and ammunition were detected. Four of them were convicted in May 1987, their excuse being that 'the weapons were for the defence of Irish Catholic households'.

By the mid-1980s, the PIRA itself was getting short of arms, having lost the majority of the previously mentioned '5,000', as Security Forces on both sides of the

Border persistently uncovered secret caches. The American arms supply line had failed, as owing to British pressure in America, gun-runners for the PIRA were arrested, one being Michael Flannery, of Noraid. However, in November 1984, five of them, including Flannery, were acquitted by a New York Court of conspiring to export arms to the IRA in Ireland, by claiming the Central Intelligence Agency (CIA) had secretly approved of their plans.

The vital importance of shipments to the 'war effort' meant that they continued to be undertaken despite the risks involved. During September 1984, in a joint American-British-Irish intelligence operation, an arms cargo was tracked by satellite and British Nimrod maritime reconnaissance aircraft across the Atlantic Ocean. It was monitored while being trans-shipped to a small Irish trawler, the *Marita Anne*, which was then boarded by the Irish Navy as it neared the Co Kerry coast and the crew arrested. Aboard were found 90 rifles, 60 machine-guns, 31 hand-guns, 71,000 rounds of ammunition, grenades and training manuals. Three men on board were later convicted, one being Martin Feris, a member of the PIRA Army Council. Later, in the USA, after a 12-month inquiry, in Boston, the Federal Bureau of Investigation (FBI) broke up an arms smuggling ring that was buying arms, including Soviet SAM-7s (Surface-to-Air Missiles), to ship to the IRA.

Libya was another spasmodic supplier of arms to the IRA, not always with success, as exampled by the SS *Claudia*, a ship bringing in a large cargo of weapons, by way of Cyprus. The deal is reputed to have been set up by Gerry Adams. The ship was intercepted in March (1973) by the Irish Navy off Co Waterford. However, some Libyan arms did get through in the early 1970s and later, as evidenced in January 1986 when the Gardai (Police) uncovered a cache of 140 Kalashnikov automatic rifles in boxes, stamped 'Libyan Armed Forces'.

The heaviest blow of all to the Libyan connection came in October 1987, when French Customs officers boarded a Panamanian-registered ship, the *Eksund*, off Brest, which had been tracked for some days. It had loaded arms at Tripoli, Libya, and the cargo consisted of 20 SAM-7s (the long sought after weapon), and 1,000 Kalashnikov automatic rifles, ten heavy 12.7mm anti-aircraft guns, 600 grenades, 50 tons of ammunition, and two tons of 'Semtex' explosives. The PIRA had planned to land these arms by night on remote parts of the eastern Irish coastline, and distribute them to prepared secret caches, ready for a major offensive in 1988.

The five men aboard the *Eksund* were taken into custody; the most important person aboard was Gabriel Cleary, the PIRA's Chief Logistics Officer, having the rank of Quartermaster, and one of its few expert bomb-makers still at large. Cleary had booby-trapped the cargo, but being caught by surprise by the French, was unable to activate the device in time, and so sink the ship. He had been sent on the trip to assess the quality and condition of the weapons obtained. He had only appeared before an Irish Court once, charged with possession of explosives, but had been released for lack of evidence; although he had long been under Gardai surveillance, and when he disappeared it was assumed he had gone to England.

PIRA innovations continued, and another appeared in January 1988, being used against a lightly armoured RUC Land Rover, killing one policeman and injuring two others in Belfast. This became known as the 'Droge impact-grenade', which was a stick-handled grenade, packed with Semtex explosives, its copper head concentrating the force of the explosion at the point of impact. The 'droge' was a tiny parachute-like apparatus that opened in flight to ensure the grenade struck at the right angle. This meant that RUC armour-protected vehicles would have to be strengthened.

Discipline Despite British claims to the contrary, there were several 'No-Go' areas in parts of NI, into which RUC personnel could only penetrate in force, and often only with Army assistance, which meant they were unable fully to carry out their normal police functions. The PIRA had stepped into this police void in such districts, holding the people within them hostage, administering its own rough form of justice which ranged from 'execution by the bullet' for informers (the age-old curse of Irish dissident organizations), and 'knee-capping' for non-compliance with PIRA orders; to dropping blocks of concrete on hands or feet.

At a rally in April 1983, a Provisional Sinn Fein leader stated that 'knee-capping' would no longer be a punishment, and that persuasion would be used instead. It is true that the spate lessened, but they continued, according to RUC records, to average about 30 annually. There was a sudden resurgence in 1987, when 124 were officially recorded, mainly for offences committed by young people, as something of a crime wave had developed in No-Go areas in the absence of normal policing. This seemed to be quite acceptable, at least on the surface, to a majority of the RC population, which regarded it as a lesser, but necessary evil, to keep a semblance of order and deter crime. Belfast surgeons had become adept at repairing shattered limb joints. The PIRA also inflicted 'humiliation' punishments on 'social offenders' such as street-cleaning and garbage removal.

In 1985, when financial problems came to a head, four 'hawks' in the PIRA Army Council, demanded that the expensive political struggle be abandoned, and all money available be devoted to the 'armed struggle'. All were senior PIRA veterans; they were Ivor Bell, a former CO of the Belfast Brigade; Anthony Murray, who had led the 'RPG-7 ASUs'; Eddie Carmichael, a former brigade commander; and Anne Doyle, a PIRA courier. Gerry Adams, then advocating the 'Armalite rifle and the ballot box' strategy, as (assumed) Chief of Staff, won the day; Bill McKee, the Adjutant-General, responsible for internal discipline, and other Army Council members, rallied to him. The four protesters were dismissed from the PIRA completely, and warned they would be 'executed' if they caused any trouble.

Tactics At the beginning of the decade the PIRA was using its newly formed ASUs mainly for hit-and-run operations, avoiding head-on clashes with the Security Forces. They concentrated on explosions that could be detonated by either timing devices or remote control, and afforded a good chance of escape. The object was to keep up pressure against the Army and the RUC; in the years 1980–83 inclusive, 1,839 'shootings' and 897 'explosions' were officially recorded by the RUC; while from 1984–1987 there were 1,346 shootings and 533 explosions, a considerable total tail-off.

As the Security Forces improved their counter-terrorism measures, including forensic detection techniques, the PIRA also moved with the times. Few, if any, PIRA activists habitually carried arms of any sort, either in NI or the ROI, because of severe penalties if caught. Arms and explosives were kept in secret caches, briefly taken out for a particular operation, and then hurriedly returned. Volunteers were sent for, given their orders, weapons, and a change of clothing. After the exploit, they returned the weapons and borrowed clothing, were debriefed, and returned to their normal habitat without any tell-tale traces of explosives or weapons to incriminate them; they were 'forensically clean'.

Operations Most PIRA terrorist-related incidents were small, designed to maintain the tempo of suspense with the occasional dramatic major exploit to catch media headlines. During 1984, for example, a year in which 64 people were killed, and 866 injured in terrorist-related violence, perhaps the most notorious incident occurred in September, when a car-bomb exploded in Newry, injuring 72 people, and devastating an entire street.

One of the most spectacular exploits committed by the PIRA, took place in Enniskillen, on Remembrance Sunday, in November 1987, when Loyalists assembled and marched in Honour of the Dead of the two world wars. At 10.45 hours, as the parade, which included youth organizations, was forming up in the town centre, a bomb near them exploded, killing eleven people and injuring more than 60, including women and children. The West Fermanagh Brigade of the PIRA claimed responsibility. The Enniskillen explosion obtained wide media publicity, as home video cameras on the spot to record the ceremonies, vividly filmed the devastation, the rescuing of wounded, the many trapped under debris, and the recovering of dead from beneath heaps of rubble. It resulted in waves of horror, not only in the United Kingdom but in the Republic too. The public were appalled at such wantonly indiscriminate slaughter of civilians. Some wondered whether Gerry Adams was losing his seemingly absolute authority over Republican affairs, or whether some maverick ASU leader had acted on his own initiative. Belatedly, the PIRA made allegations that the Security Forces had detonated the bomb prematurely with their 'radio clearance equipment'. The Security Forces denied this, but admitted they did have what they called their 'agile chimp', which could detect detonators at a distance, and could also alter timing detonators; but insisted they always cleared potential danger areas before they used it.

The Enniskillen act was only half of an attempted double; a remote-control beer-keg bomb had been placed in a ditch at the border village of Tullyhommon, eighteen miles away. It failed to explode, thus narrowly averting another outrage against an assembling Remembrance Day Parade.

PIRA Intimidation The PIRA have always tried to intimidate those under its influence from working for the Security Forces in NI, but with only limited success; if RCs would not do the jobs required, non-RCs would – the unemployment rate being high. In August 1986, the PIRA extended its threats, saying that anyone involved in administration, maintenance or construction work at Army or RUC installations, would become legitimate targets for assassination. The terrorist net was gradually widened to include contractors, and even those supplying milk to police stations. Four contractors were killed in 1985; the first victim of this new PIRA tactic was an electrician in Londonderry who was shot dead, and a few weeks later another building worker was killed. These incidents did not stop non-RCs working as usual in their own community areas, but did have an effect elsewhere. Military engineers and Royal Pioneer Corps personnel had to be brought in for essential government building maintenance requirements.

Bandit Country Despite denials by the Irish Government, the IRA were able to use the ROI as a sanctuary, although sometimes it was an uncertain one. The terrorists were aided by the fact that the border was completely 'open', its 316 miles often cutting throught farms and fields and even dwellings. There were few official 'check points', and many 'unapproved roads', that traversed the demarcation line, unmanned and unmarked. Large stretches of territory in the North adjacent to the border had a Catholic population, and became known as 'Bandit Country' since the Queen's Writ ran only spasmodically and imperfectly. Most terrorist acts in this hostile area, and even farther afield, were committed by IRA activists who crossed into NI from the ROI for this specific purpose, quickly returning again, to live quite openly in relative security.

In the Bandit Country of South Armagh some police posts had become fortified joint Army-RUC bases, amid a hostile population, often supplied and reinforced by helicopter, such as the often photographed (by the media) one at Crossmaglen. Security Forces used helicopters extensively for both operational mobility and logistic purposes. There was no direct contact between the armed forces of Britain and the ROI, and only sparse liaison between respective Police Chiefs.

It was not until the discovery of Libyan arms in the Republic, and the incident of the *Eksund*, which was carrying sophisticated weaponry that the Irish Army did not possess, that the Irish Government was jolted into a more co-operative attitude. In November 1987 the newly appointed Gardai Chief, Eamon Doherty, was ordered to liaise directly with the Chief Constable of the RUC on cross-border security; and the first such meeting for three years took place. During November and December, there were massive and intensive searches for arms on both sides since neither forces could be absolutely sure that some Libyan arms had not already been landed either in the north or the south. A few small caches were unearthed, but the SOI authorities were amazed at the large, purpose-built bunkers they discovered lying empty waiting to receive quantities of weaponry.

Loyalist Para-militaries

Opposed to the Republicans in NI were a number of Loyalist para-military groups that had sprung into existence during the present period of sectarian strife. They carried out assassinations and reprisal raids on the IRA and RC communities. The IRA replied in kind. Loyalist groups did not have quite the same degree of freedom and security, as did the IRA, snug within RC communities, being harried by the RUC in the interests of law and order.

One Loyalist group was the Ulster Volunteer Force (UVF), whose traditions went back to the days of 1912, and the violent demands for Home Rule by Protestant northerners which, after falling into abeyance, was revived in 1969 when the Union seemed to be threatened. Proscribed in 1975, it continued its terrorist activities underground, until its momentum declined after a number of its leaders were arrested in 1983.

Another was the Ulster Defence Association (UDA) which came into being in September 1971, under the leadership of Andy Tyrie, as a grouping of street defence associations taking on vigilante tasks. Its strength quickly rose to a maximum of some 50,000 volunteers, and it did much to break the provisional 'power-sharing' administration in 1974. By 1980, its membership had declined to 12,000 or so, and internal difficulties were disrupting the movement. A more violent group was the Ulster Freedom Fighters (UFF), which had splintered from the UDA, though the dividing line was fine; it concentrated upon sectarian murders. Generally, most Loyalist terrorist groups were fairly inactive during the first part of the decade, but most sprang to life again after November 1985, when the Anglo-Irish

Agreement (Hillsborough Accord) came into operation, which for the first time gave the Dublin government some say in NI affairs.

Sectarian Warfare Sectarian tit-for-tat assassinations continued spasmodically; in October 1982, Thomas Cochrane, an Ulster Defence Regiment (UDR) member, was kidnapped by the PIRA. Later the same day, Joseph Donegan, a Roman Catholic, was kidnapped by the UVF and he was beaten to death in retaliation.

A month later the IRA ambushed Lennie Murphy, known as 'the Shankhill Butcher', and reputed leader of the UVF. The PIRA stated that Murphy had been 'executed' as he was held responsible for the murder of '20 innocent Nationalists'; and that he had been planning to establish a Loyalist 'terrorist team'. It was alleged that Murphy had been 'set-up' by his own men, in collusion with PIRA racketeers, over the division of territory for 'protection' purposes. The bodies of three RCs were found in ensuing weeks in the area.

In NI religion is often a convenient label to differentiate between two antagonistic political viewpoints. Generally, the clergy of both RC and non-RC denominations avoid direct involvement with terrorist groups, piously confining themselves to condemning violence and cautioning moderation, while defending their flocks' respective Republican and Loyalist ideals. This has meant they have not been seen as 'legitimate' terrorist targets; there were, however, exceptions on the Loyalist side with certain of the clergy taking on political roles and responsibilities, which brought them actively into the sectarian struggle. One was the Reverend Ian Paisley, leader of the Democratic Unionist Party (DUP), who received periodic death threats from the IRA, and often wore a flak-jacket under his coat on public occasions. Another was the Reverend Robert Bradford, a Non-Conformist Minister, Deputy Leader of the DUP, and Westminster Member of Parliament. Accused of being a 'UDA organizer', he was shot dead at a political meeting by an IRA Volunteer in November 1981. He was the first Ulster clergyman to be killed in terrorist violence during the present spate of 'troubles'.

INLA broke the unspoken 'hands off the clergy' rule, two years later in 1983, when three of its members entered the Mountain Lodge Pentecostal Hall, Darkley, Co Armagh, and fired into the congregation, killing three people and injuring others. An INLA statement, purporting to come from the 'Catholic Reaction Force', declared the act to be a 'token retaliation' for recent sectarian violence against RCs in Armagh. The DUP withdrew from the dormant Northern Ireland Assembly in protest.

The Security Forces

The British Army The British Army had been 'called out in the Aid of the Civil Power' in 1969, because the RUC lacked modern equipment and was too small to be able to counter the rising waves of violence in the Province. The 6,000 British troops already stationed there were reinforced to a maximum strength of 22,000 (in 1972), and then progressively reduced to about 11,500 by 1980. The British Army had had considerable counter-insurgency experience in several countries, including Kenya, Cyprus, Aden and Borneo. Initially, they took control of the 'Emergency', pushing the RUC aside into a secondary role, which caused some friction between the two. At first the RC population, fearing reprisals against them by the predominantly Protestant-manned RUC, and its auxiliary, the 'B-Specials'; both of which had a decidedly partisan attitude, had welcomed the arrival of British troops. Recovering from its surprise, the IRA worked to turn the RC population against the British troops, a policy that was aided by some of the 'colonial' methods they adopted originally. However, the British Army reverted to a secondary role, when an enlarged and retrained RUC, was able to take control as the paramount civilian police force; providing it with military support when required, guarding certain installations, and patrolling Bandit Country.

A central IRA demand was 'British Troops Out'; it consistently targeted British forces in NI, setting ambushes, using car-bombs and booby-traps. The IRA seemed to want to emulate the character of the British Army, and to assume the dignity and status of being an 'army', fighting against one of the finest armies in the world. One of the most notorious incidents perpetrated by the INLA, was an explosion at the Droppin Well Bar in Ballykelly, Co Londonderry, near Shackleton Barracks. It was a frequent haunt of British Servicemen, and on 6 December 1982, a bomb exploded inside which killed seventeen people (eleven soldiers and six civilians) and injured more than 60 others. No customary warning was given to enable civilians to be evacuated from the danger zone. The INLA was proscribed in the ROI because of this exploit, and eventually four INLA members (two men and two women) were convicted for the atrocity in June 1986.

The Ulster Defence Regiment Included as part of the Security Forces in NI was the Ulster Defence Regiment (UDR), a part-time territorial unit, with an establishment of more than 6,500, making it the largest regiment in the British Army. Its tasks were mainly to patrol and guard certain areas. Personnel were recruited locally, but the proportion of RCs was tiny, and so it was seen by the IRA and the RC population as a partisan force. Volunteers, especially those who lived in 'mixed', or rural areas, were regarded as 'soft targets' for IRA terrorists, and were in especial danger when off duty. From its formation in 1970 until the end of December 1987, 168 of its members had been killed, of whom 137 were off duty; and another 49 had been killed after they had left the UDR.

The Royal Ulster Constabulary In 1980, the Royal Ulster Constabulary, the normal police force of NI, had a regular strength of just over 7,500 men (and women), and a mustered police reserve of amost 4,000 personnel. Officially, 90 per cent of its strength was non-RC, causing it to be disliked and feared by the RC communities, who regarded it as an oppressive sectarian body. It had been provided with modern policing equipment and vehicles; and sections of it were given special training in counter-insurgency tactics, some at the British SAS Depot in England, which tended to instil an aggressive attitude. Influenced by SAS methods, they tended to rely on speed in reaction and firepower – principles running counter to the normal British concept of policing.

To combat rioting and stone-throwing the RUC used rubber bullets initially and then plastic ones, some of which caused injuries and even death. This resulted in complaints, and occasionally demands for compensation. Plastic bullets were used extensively in the 'hunger-strike' period of 1981, and concern about their effect was voiced in the British Parliament. In May 1982, a motion to ban the use of plastic bullets in the European Economic Community (EEC) countries, was accepted in the European Parliament; and on 31 January 1983, the British National Council for Civil Liberties launched a campaign against their use in Britain and NI. However, these pleas were ignored, and the Army and RUC continued to use them, resulting in a number of fatalities.

Counter-Insurgency

Shoot to Kill From November 1982 until April 1983, ten people were shot dead in suspicious circumstances by the Security Forces. The Provisional Sinn Fein, the Social Democratic and Labour Party (SDLP), and the RC clergy, all protested, claiming that a 'shoot-to-kill' policy was in operation. They called for a public inquiry, but the Secretary of State denied that such a deliberate policy existed; although he confirmed later in Parliament that 'Special Units' were operating with the specific task of dealing with terrorist intelligence. He was thought to be referring to the SAS 'stake-out' teams. John Hume, leader of the moderately Nationalist SDLP, claimed on 29 December, that during the two previous months, the British Army had killed seven people and wounded three, alleging that the government had 'abandoned the rule of law'. Examples included the killing of Seamus McGrew and Roddy Carroll, both INLA members.

Controversy over the alleged British shoot-to-kill policy continued; and after the acquittal of a RUC policeman accused of shooting Seamus McGrew, it was heightened and added to by whispers that the Security Forces had operated in ROI territory. In April 1984, the British Government apologized to the Irish Government for cross-border activity and the following month, a Police Inquiry into these matters began, conducted by John Stalker, Deputy Chief Constable of Greater Manchester Police. He made an interim report in September 1985; completing Part I of his report, in May 1986, which was then handed to the Chief Constable of the RUC. It is believed Stalker had uncovered new evidence, and recommended the prosecution of certain senior officers.

Almost immediately Stalker was made to go on leave, pending investigation into alleged breaches of police discipline, unrelated to his activities in Ulster. Colin Sampson, Chief Constable of the West Yorkshire Police, was appointed to investigate allegations against Stalker, and to continue with the ongoing inquiry. This caused loud protests and allegations of a cover-up; Amnesty International urged that an open inquiry be held, as did a group of US Congressmen; John Hume said, 'Sinister forces are at work to prevent the completion of the Stalker Enquiry', while the Irish Government officially expressed 'disquiet'.

The Sampson Report on Stalker recommended that he be disciplined on several counts, but this was rejected by the Greater Manchester Police Authority, and he was then reinstated to his former position as Deputy Chief Constable. Part II of the inquiry (now by Sampson), was delivered to the Chief Constable of the RUC in March 1987 and the decision not to publish it caused general protest. In January 1988, it was announced that there would be no prosecutions emanating from the Stalker-Sampson Report.

The Loughgall Ambush British SAS personnel were frequently employed on covert operations too, notably in Bandit Country, and these 'Eagle Patrols' were put down by helicopter often at night, and then picked up again, after their 'stake-out and surveillance' missions or ambushes. Also, at intervals, 40-feet-high observation towers had been erected to monitor ground movement. During 1987, the PIRA policy was to intimidate the RUC, and force it to remove its presence from Bandit Country, concentrating first on the small police stations, usually manned only part-time. The PIRA had made one successful experiment previously; using a bull-dozer, carrying a bomb on its shovel, to break down the outer metal fencing then detonating the bomb by remote-control. Afterwards they would intimidate workmen to prevent the station being re-built or repaired.

On 8 May 1987, Patrick Kelly, CO of the East Tyrone Brigade, mustered and deployed his ASU, of eight men, one of whom was Jim Lynagh, a top PIRA gunman. A bull-dozer was hijacked, and a metal beer keg, packed with explosives, loaded on to it, which with three men aboard, set off followed by a van carrying the other five terrorists. It was to be a simple hit-and-run raid in daylight, the object being to destroy Loughgall Police Station, Co Armagh, and kill any RUC personnel who happened to be inside.

An informer alerted the Security Forces, and a mixed team of British SAS soldiers and members of the RUC Special Unit, prepared an ambush into which, unwittingly, the PIRA ASU drove head-first. At about 19.30 hours the ASU reached its target, the bull-dozer crashed through the outer fencing, and the bomb was exploded, ripping open the building. Instantly, fire was opened by the ambush party, and in a gun-battle lasting about ten minutes, all eight PIRA men were killed. One of the dead was Patrick McKearney, a Maze Prison escapee. Two policemen and a soldier were injured; one civilian in a car was also killed by the Security Forces, and his companion was injured. The SAS had ringed the area, and had mistaken the car for a terrorist back-up vehicle; but a number of school girls, playing in a school building some 300 yards away, were unhurt.

The 'Loughgall Ambush' was quickly turned into the 'Loughgall Massacre' for propaganda purposes, but was one of the most disastrous defeats the PIRA had suffered for many years. It demonstrated that Security Forces could still obtain good information from informers, and that despite bland official statements to the contrary, a shoot-to-kill policy existed. Gerry Adams philosophically commented, 'The IRA Volunteers would have understood the risk they were taking'. Informers remained the curse of the IRA, and during the early part of 1987 the whole of the command staff of the Belfast Brigade, about 20 people, was abruptly moved to other posts in an attempt to discover a highly placed 'mole'.

Gibraltar: A Pre-Emptive Strike Brilliant surveillance and co-operation between British, Spanish and Gibraltarean Security Forces, caused another serious PIRA failure when, on 6 March 1988 in Gibraltar, British SAS soldiers shot dead three terrorists (Mairead Farrall, Sean Savage and Daniel McCann) who were preparing a car-bomb to be exploded in the small central square during the traditional ceremony of Changing the Guard, usually watched by a large crowd of tourists and locals. The Spanish police found the car-bomb at Marbella, some 40 miles from Gibraltar. Approximately 220 pounds of Semtex explosive had been wired up to a timing detonator (but not primed), set for 11.40 hours (when the ceremony would be ending).

Led by Mairead Farrell, this PIRA ASU, which also included another female (never apprehended), had been under Spanish police surveillance for about four months. Experts said that had the car-bomb been put in position and detonated, several hundred people would have been killed, maimed or injured in the confined space around the site of the Ceremony which proceeded normally on the 8th.

Locals refused to handle the coffins containing the bodies of the terrorists, and no Irish Airline would transport them back to Ireland, so a British civil aircraft had to be chartered, and British soldiers loaded the coffins aboard. The coffins were landed at Dublin Airport, and then moved in a slow 'triumphal procession' by road to Belfast. The funeral was held at Milltown Cemetery, on the 16th, when mourners were attacked by a lone terrorist. More 'martyrs' had been added to the Republican Movement's mythical tradition.

Violence at Funerals Rowdy demonstrations often occurred at IRA funerals, usually when the RUC tried to prevent masked PIRA activists firing revolver shots over coffins in the military manner, and when RUC members tried to snatch the Republican tricolour flag from coffins. In March 1987, at the funeral near Belfast of a RUC member who had been killed by a booby-trap, bombs exploded on the route just before the funeral cortege was due to pass, six people being injured. A PIRA statement, admitting responsibility, said. 'If you want to bury your dead, then keep a dignified distance from Republican and Nationalist funerals.'

During the following month, there were rowdy, hostile demonstrations at the funeral of Lawrence Marley, a leading PIRA member in Belfast, who had been killed by the UVF. It had to be postponed twice because the RUC were determined to prevent the PIRA gunmen rushing forward to fire shots over the coffin. Bishop Daly, of Derry, banned requiem masses for terrorists, but not all the RC clergy took the same sharp line.

March 1988 was an unfortunate month for funerals in the Province. On the 16th, crowds were massed and marshalled by PIRA stewards at Milltown Cemetery, West Belfast, the RUC adopting an 'unobtrusive presence' in the background, for the funeral of three IRA members who had been shot by the British Special Air Service Regiment (SAS) in Gibraltar. As the coffins were being lowered into the ground, a lone Protestant terrorist, who had mingled with the crowds, threw three grenades at the graveside mourners, and then fired a number of pistol shots, killing three people and injuring 50. The assassin, identified as Michael Stone, was probably a UDA member (although the UDA denied this). He attempted to escape but was caught and beaten, before a fortunate rescue by the RUC.

The next horrific incident occurred at the same cemetery several days later during the funeral of a PIRA member who had been killed on the 16th. Again, this funeral was attended by huge crowds organized by PIRA stewards; two British soldiers, in plain clothes in an unmarked car, blundered into the funeral procession, were detected and dragged from the car then severely beaten and killed. This event was filmed in some detail by television cameramen present, and shown in Britain, and world-wide, evoking a storm of revulsion and horror.

The Secretary of State ordered an immediate inquiry into RUC policing arrangements for PIRA funerals. These events were seen as a setback for the Chief Constable's new policy of trying to create a reputation of fairness and impartiality for his Force, as he had laid down in his *Professional Policing Ethics*, a 13-point code of conduct. He claimed it was beginning to have a good effect, and quoted a province-wide opinion poll, in which 72 per cent of the people polled indicated that they thought the 'RUC was doing a good job'.

The Supergrass System One of the biggest problems in bringing terrorists to justice in any country is a lack of witnesses to give evidence against them in open Court. Witnesses would probably be killed, and perhaps tortured first, by their former comrades. This affected NI, where there was no shortage of informers. Beginning in 1981, large cash rewards, immunity from prosecution, a new identity, and tickets out of NI for themselves and their families, were incentives dangled before those who stood to be imprisoned for many years for their crimes. Several individuals accepted, and thereby became 'Supergrasses'. The system was reputed to have been started by Sir Maurice Oldfield, a former MI6 Chief, brought out of retirement in 1979, as Co-ordinator of Security Forces in NI, to bring about an improvement in relations between the Army and the RUC. Oldfield is said to have had discussions about the Supergrass system with certain of the RC clergy, and to have sought its support; something that is now vehemently denied.

The first Supergrass trial, of which there were a number, ended on 11 April 1983, when fourteen Loyalists, mainly UVF members, were convicted of 60 terrorist-related crimes on the evidence of one man, Joseph Bennet, who claimed to be the CO of the UVF detachment in Belfast. Other supergrasses whose names became well-known, include Henry Kirkpatrick (INLA), Raymond Gilmour (PIRA), Christopher Black (PIRA), Keven McGrady (PIRA), William Allan (UVF), and one woman, Angela Whoriskey (PIRA): there were others.

In his Annual Report of 1982, the Chief Constable of the RUC stated that the 'emergence of converted terrorists' was the most significant factor of the year; and by 1984, he was reporting that 30 informers had given information leading to the arrest and conviction of more than 500 people. This was a severe blow to terrorist groups, both Republican and Loyalist.

Whenever possible, terrorist groups wreaked their own vengeance; for example, the INLA 'executed' Eric Daly in May 1983; and the PIRA 'executed' Brian McNally, in July the following year. Also, terrorist groups put what pressure they could on families of supergrasses (who themselves were invariably held in protective custody for their own safety), even kidnapping and threatening to kill relatives unless they recanted their evidence. Many supergrasses succumbed to these threats, and defendants then had to be released wholesale.

Many convicted terrorists were later released on appeal owing to doubts as to the veracity of supergrass evidence, as many old scores were paid. Defendants were usually held in custody awaiting trial for long periods while evidence was being processed, and neither the British Government, nor the legal profession liked the system at all. The NI Secretary constantly asserted that his Department had not been involved in the supergrass decision, but he did claim its use accounted for the decline in terrorism in the Province. In October 1986 another trial was abandoned, being the sixteenth to fail since 1981; there came a pause in the supergrass system.

A 'confidential telephone' system had been established by the RUC, back in 1972, when members of the public were encouraged to ring certain numbers displayed in telephone call-boxes, and pass on information to the police in confidence and anonymity. This was considered to be a moderate success. In Belfast alone, during 1985, there were 800 such calls; this increased the following year to more than 3,000, of which about 10 per cent were concerned with terrorist-related crimes. The number of telephone lines for this service was increased to capitalize on the flow of intelligence it was yielding.

Cross-Border Co-operation Extradition problems continued to plague the British Government in its efforts to bring terrorists to justice. The open Border was a source of frustration to the RUC, who complained that some 150 'known' IRA terrorists were living in freedom in the ROI, beyond its reach; and that Irish Courts were reluctant to extradite them, or convict them locally on RUC evidence. This had been true to a large extent for a long time; but it was also true that more than 100 IRA terrorists were in Irish prisons or detention.

The (Irish) Criminal Law Jurisdiction Act, and the analogous (British) Prevention of Terrorism Act (both of 1976), catering for the extradition of terrorists, or their trial in whichever country they were found, only began to work (creakingly) in the early 1980s; and then difficulties were often made in extradition proceedings, with Irish complaints that RUC evidence was insufficient. Dominic McGlinchey (then believed to be Head of the INLA) was the first terrorist to be extradited from the ROI, in 1982, the Chief Justice ruling that his offences were not political. He had been captured by the Gardai, but jumped bail in NI. The European Suppression of Terrorism Convention (of 1977) had similar extradition, and venue of trial, clauses, but was not signed by the ROI Government until February 1986.

Few foreign countries made extradition of IRA terrorists easy, as most had traditions of political asylum, or political reasons for not complying. In 1984, a New York Court ruled that Joseph Doherty, a Crumlin Road Prison escapee wanted for involvement in the M-60 Murder, could not be extradited because his crime was 'political in character'. However, the US-British Extradition Treaty of 1985 was specifically drafted so that serious criminal offenders could not put forward a 'political excuse'. After a slow start, this Treaty began to work reasonably well and did pull in a few long-term IRA refugees. Some foreign countries were more amenable than others; in October 1986, a Dutch Court approved the extradition to the United Kingdom, of Gerard Kelly and Brendan McFarlane, both Maze escapees, but made it conditional that they would only face 'escaping' charges.

The Dual Strategy for Revolution

Gerry Adams Intelligent, vocal, articulate and shrewd, Gerry Adams has often been referred to as the 'respectable face of terrorism'; to the RUC he is known as 'Mr PIRA'. Without doubt he is probably the most influential man in Republican circles in this decade. Born in Belfast in 1949, now married with a teen-aged son, he is steeped in Republican ideals and traditions; he became an IRA activist at an early age. Interned in 1971, he was important enough then to be included in the IRA groups flown to London to engage in secret talks with the British Government. In NI he rose to command the Belfast Brigade (which his brother Paddy now probably commands), and then gained a seat on the Army Council as the Director of Procurement.

When Chief of Staff Twomey was arrested in Dublin in 1973, Adams probably acted in his stead until Twomey was snatched from prison to resume his appointment. The two men worked together to change the old military-style PIRA into an effective secret organization. Arrested in 1978, Adams was released on the technicality that membership of the Sinn Fein did not automatically mean he was a member of the IRA. Previously, senior IRA appointments were open secrets, but now they are 'Top Secret'. Adams dominates the PIRA Army Council, but his precise appointment is uncertain. His oft-repeated comments that' 'I am not in the IRA, and have never been in the IRA,' provoke either amused, or cynical smiles.

On the other hand, his position on the Provisional Sinn Fein Council is quite clear; he was elected President in November 1983, in place of Rory O'Brady, who probably stepped down because of age and failing health. In his acceptance speech, Adams said, 'Violence by freedom fighters is the only force likely to affect British Government policy,' which initially endeared him to the 'Hawks'. Martin

McGuiness became Deputy President; and is probably now Chief of Staff of the PIRA.

The Ballot Box and the Armalite For some time Adams had been developing his policy of the 'Ballot Box and the Armalite'. He believed that the Republican movement needed a broad political base to widen the struggle, and that violence alone was insufficient to achieve it; he concluded that Provisional Sinn Fein should vigorously enter the political arena, in both NI and the ROI. He preached his ideas in articles written for the Provisional Sinn Fein newspaper, *Republician News*, under the pen-name of 'Brownie', views that did not appeal to certain other PIRA leaders.

Standing as a Provisional Sinn Fein candidate in the British general election of June 1983, Adams won the constituency of West Belfast, but did not take his seat at Westminster. On 15 May 1985, for the first time in many years, under Adams's guidance, the Provisional Sinn Fein took part in Province-wide elections, winning 59 (out of 566) seats, and obtaining 12 per cent of the votes cast.

Adams had his enemies, especially in Loyalist para-military groups, and when leaving a Belfast Court, on 14 May 1984, where he was facing charges of obstruction, he and three companions were shot and wounded by a Loyalist UFF gang.

Gerry Adams also sought contacts with terrorist groups in Europe, notably the West German RAF which had claimed involvement in certain acts of terrorism against British Army personnel and installations on the Continent. While there may have been some substance in them, most of these claims were doubtful. However, three British Servicemen were killed and three seriously wounded in two incidents on 1 May 1988 in Dutch villages close to the West German border; one being a car-bomb explosion and the other a shooting incident. Holland had gained a dubious reputation as a haven for IRA activists and fugitives.

The Five Demands Despite the plethora of terrorism in the early part of the decade, media attention tended to focus on prison protests and hunger-strikes. Since 1978, an average of up to 400 IRA prisoners had been 'On the Blanket', insisting upon the implementation of what had become known as the 'Five Demands'. These included political status, and the right to wear their own clothes. Refusing to wear prison uniform, they had only a prison blanket with which to drape themselves; it was linked to the 'Dirty Protest' where prisoners refused to use lavatories, and smeared excreta on cell walls, which had to be frequently steam-hosed down.

Hunger-Strikes On 27 October 1980, seven prisoners (six PIRA and one INLA) went on hunger-strike to obtain the Five Demands, at the Maze Prison, near Belfast, but this was called off after 53 days, when it became clear that it was having no effect on an implacable British Government. Three IRA women prisoners, held in Armagh women's prison, also called off a similar hunger-strike.

This was followed by a further series of hunger-strikes in 1981, in the 'H Block', at the Maze Prison, in which ten hunger-strikes died. The first was Bobby Sands, who began his hunger-strike on 1 March; and he was joined by others. The object was to pressure the British Government into acceding to the Five Demands, but it remained adamant in refusal. While on hunger-strike, Sands was elected to the vacant Parliamentary seat of Fermanagh and South Tyrone. This was a departure from normal IRA practice of not acknowledging the authority of the British Crown, and of not taking part in British democratic processes. Sands died on 5 May; and the world's media watched transfixed as one by one the other hunger-strikers also died.

The last to die was Michael Devine, a founder-member of INLA, on 20 August. An INLA spokesman stated that Devine would not be replaced, as the hunger-strike was not proving to be an effective weapon; adding that if it was 'all our prisoners would be dead in six months'. Thirteen prisoners had already abandoned their hunger-strikes for one reason or another; six continued, but they too gave up on 3 October when their families agreed that they should be given medical attention when they became unconscious, which made their ordeal pointless.

Afterwards, however, certain prison reforms were quickly put into effect, including allowing prisoners to wear their own clothes; and as IRA prisoners received them from their familites the 'Blanket' and 'Dirty' protests gradually tailed off, to terminate by the end of October. The British Government had achieved a considerable victory over terrorism, but it tended to be double-edged, as the hunger-strike ordeal had generated an enthusiasm and determination that did much to reinforce the IRA terrorist campaign in the months and years ahead; also, the Five Demands were all but conceded. During the March-October hunger-strike period tension had run very high in the Province; protest marches and demonstrations were mounted by Republicans, and incidents of IRA terrorism increased. This caused the government to fly in 600 'Spearhead' (stand-by) troops to reinforce the British garrison. In May, for example, in several incidents ten people were killed including six soldiers.

Prison Escapes The annual toll of death, injury and destruction had become commonplace, barely attracting British public attention to any great degree. However, the media always showed interest in escapees from prison, in which the IRA had an impressive record dating from De Valera's break-out from Lincoln Gaol in 1919, to Seamus Twomey, Chief-of-Staff of the PIRA, being lifted to freedom by a helicopter from the exercise yard at Mountjoy Prison, Dublin in August 1973. More recently, eight IRA terrorists on remand in the Crumlin Road Prison, Belfast, facing charges of being involved in what had become known as the 'M-60 Murder', the killing of an SAS officer with that type of American machine-gun, all escaped in June 1981.

This event was surpassed when a well-planned mass escape of 38 IRA prisoners was made on 25 September 1983, from the Maze Prison (where in November 1974, 32 IRA prisoners had tunnelled their way to freedom). Within the perimeter of the Maze, a former army camp, were eight 'H Blocks', so-called from the shape of the plan of the buildings, each surrounded by its own security fence. In H-7 Block were 126 prisoners, guarded by 24 prison officers. Five revolvers, some ammunition and two replica revolvers had been smuggled in. At 14.30 hours, on that Sunday afternoon, the prison officers were over-powered, tied up, and some of them stripped of their uniforms, which the prisoners donned.

When the routine 'kitchen truck' arrived bringing food from the central cook-house, it was seized, the escapees clambered aboard, and it was driven towards the main entrance. There was a scuffle between prison officers on duty there, and prisoners in officers' uniforms, during which one officer was killed and another badly injured. The main gates were then unlocked and the escapees fled to freedom. Emergency drills were slow to swing into operation, but nineteen escapees were rounded-up within hours and most of the rest with in a few months. The subsequent Hennessay Report, by the Chief Inspector of HM Prisons, was critical, high-lighting negligence and poor morale. The Prison Governor resigned. The Deputy Governor was shot dead near his home, on 6 March 1984, by the PIRA, which accused him of beating prisoners and allocating them degrading jobs.

Taking Terror to the Mainland

IRA attention very often turned to England in the belief that 'one explosion in England is worth one hundred in Northern Ireland'. Generally, the IRA avoided committing terrorist crimes in Scotland and Wales, on the grounds that the inhabitants were fellow gaels, with similar aspirations for independence, but it had periodically mounted terrorist campaigns in England. In the previous decade PIRA ASUs had based themselves amid Irish immigrant communities, but had come up against the eternal informer problem. The new policy was for ASUs to stay away from such surroundings, making them harder to track down.

During 1981, the PIRA carried out five bombing attacks in the London area. The first was on 10 October, when a bomb in a stationary laundry van, near the entrance to Chelsea Barracks, exploded as a bus carrying Irish Guardsmen, was passing. It killed two passers-by and injured more than 40 others. This was the first use outside NI of the radio-controlled detonator; previously timing devices had been used in England. A woman was seen to push the laundry van into position; she became known as the 'Blonde Bomber'; but it is thought that this was Evelyn Glenholmes, a top PIRA terrorist, wearing a wig. The other prime suspect was John Downey.

On the 17th, a car-bomb explosion, detonated by the 'tilt', or 'trembler' principle, seriously injured the Commandant General of the Royal Marines outside his home. On the 26th, a Metropolitan Police Bomb Disposal expert was killed while dealing with a device in a Wimpey Bar in Oxford Street, which had been booby-trapped; the first touch activated the trembler causing an instant explosion. Bombs were also found in several London departmental stores, but all were made safe. The PIRA claimed this series of bombing incidents was its answer to the widespread use of plastic bullets in NI during the hunger-strike period.

In November the PIRA Army Council warned that it would escalate bombing in England; on the 11th, there were two explosions at the home of the Attorney General, who happened to be away at the time, and no one was hurt. On the 23rd, a booby-trapped toy pistol injured two women and a dog outside Woolwich Barracks. Eventually, in March 1985, two terrorists, Thomas Quigley and Paul Kavanagh, were convicted of the Chelsea Barracks bombing incident, and involvement in others in the London area.

Hyde Park and Harrods There was a lengthy lull before the next major PIRA bombing exploit in London occurred on 20 July, when a remote-controlled car-bomb, packed with nails and bolts, exploded on the South Carriage Road, Hyde Park, as a mounted detachment of Household Cavalry rode past, killing four soldiers and seven horses. About two hours later, a timing device exploded under the bandstand in Regent's Park, where a military band was giving a lunch-time concert; another seven soldiers were killed. In these two incidents 51 people were injured.

More than a year later, in December 1983, London was targeted again; on the 10th, a bomb exploded at Woolwich Barracks, injuring five people, and although the Scottish National Liberation Army claimed responsibility, the device had all the hall-marks of the PIRA. On the 13th, a similar bomb, discovered in a busy South Kensington Street, was defuzed. The next exploit, on the 17th, was the worst so far;

at the height of the Christmas shopping period a car-bomb exploded outside Harrods, the department store, killing two police officers and three civilians, and injuring more than 90 people.

This indiscriminate killing and injuring of innocent people caused a well of resentment to rise against the IRA, with demands that Provisional Sinn Fein, then in Annual Convention in Dublin, be banned in NI. On the 18th, the PIRA issued a statement, claiming responsibility for the outrage, but explaining that it had not been authorized by the Army Council and that there would be 'no repetition of this type of operation'. ASU leaders had a degree of discretion, and could use their initiative to engage opportunity targets. The NI Secretary appealed to American citizens to stop assisting Noraid, which he said was funding such violence, rather than caring for the families of prisoners.

The Brighton Bombing On 12 October 1984, a date again coinciding with the Provisional Sinn Fein Annual Convention in Dublin, a 20-pound device wrecked part of the Grand Hotel in Brighton, where the Annual Conservative Party Conference was being held. The Prime Minister and several of her Cabinet Ministers were staying at the hotel. She escaped injury, but five people were killed, and 30 others injured. It had been a bold PIRA attempt to wipe out the British Cabinet. The PIRA had never forgiven the Prime Minister for her attitude during its hunger-strike period, and this incident indicated a new addition to IRA capability – the technological expertise to plant devices with long delays on the timers, meaning bombs could be planted months ahead of their intended detonation time. A real security headache.

Responsibility was instantly claimed by the PIRA, which telephoned a statement to the Radio Telefis Eireann (RTE) in Dublin, saying that, 'Today, we were unlucky, but remember, we have only to be lucky once; you have to be lucky always.' Gerry Adams said, 'The Brighton Bombing is an inevitable result of the British presence in this country.' Nearly two years later in June 1986 Patrick Magee, and five accomplices were convicted of involvement in the Brighton incident, and others.

Other PIRA ASUs remained in England, planning to explode bombs at various seaside holiday resorts during the 1985 summer season, but were thwarted by the Security Forces. One bomb, planted in the Rubens Hotel, near Buckingham Palace, was detected on 21 June, and defuzed. According to a Scotland Yard statement it had been timed to 'go off days in the future'.

Master Bomb-Makers By this time half-a-dozen or so PIRA bomb-makers had reached a high degree of sophistication, being able to assemble various types of detonators, including a timer, that could be activated over any period from four minutes to 48 days. A major triumph for the Security Forces was the arrest of Gilbert McNamee, one of the PIRA's top bomb-makers, who had most probably assembled all the bombs planted in England since 1981. A native of Crossmaglen, unlike most of his contemporaries he had gone on to further education, eventually graduating in physics at Queen's University, Belfast. Joining the PIRA, he worked as an electrician just across the ROI border, producing sophisticated detonators and explosive devices, which were taken to the ASUs in England by couriers on trawlers.

MaNamee had only appeared once before the Courts, in Dublin in 1978, accused of illegal possession of a large quantity of explosives, but he had been acquitted on a technicality. He had long been suspected, but proof was wanting.

Eventually British Security Forces located three PIRA caches of bomb materials in woodlands in England, with his incriminating finger-prints on them. McNamee was picked up in NI, ostensibly for questioning, but in fact to obtain his finger-prints; he was then released again. Once his finger-prints had been matched with those on the bomb materials, and found to be identical, he was re-arrested in August 1987, brought to London, and convicted in October. The police comment was, 'Science had trapped the scientific bomb-maker'.

Natalino Vella, an Italian icecream seller living in Dublin, not a PIRA member but employed by it on a casual, courier, basis, was arrested and convicted in London in March 1985; later in April 1987, veteran PIRA member, 60-year old Michael McKenny, who organized the courier route to England, and had the rank of Quartermaster, was also arrested and convicted. It was claimed that the British-based ASUs had been smashed, but this remains to be seen.

Disintegration of the INLA

Once more than 100 strong, the supergrass system had seriously depleted the ranks of the INLA, and the first wave of arrests in 1982 had included Gerard Steenson, its then Chief of Staff. Other senior members were progressively picked up by the RUC including Dominic McGlinchey, who had deserted the PIRA for the INLA, and forced his way upwards to become INLA Chief of Staff, crushing an internal feud in early 1984. McGlinchey tried to assassinate members of the Loyalist DUP, and had organized the Darkley Raid, but he was arrested in the ROI in March 1984, and convicted of terrorist offences. INLA then dissolved into a confused tangle of ambitious men seeking the leadership.

Failure of the Kirkpatrick Supergrass Trial led to the release of 24 INLA defendants on Christmas Eve, 1985; they included Steenson and other leaders who all rushed back to re-assume their former appointments, only to run into opposition. INLA had divided into four factions, and had almost forgotten its ideological purpose, being mostly entirely engaged in criminal activities. Led by Steenson, three of these factions, constituting the 'Army Council', offered to disband the INLA, and form a Marxist Republican political party instead. The fourth faction, which became known as the 'New GHQ', disagreed, opted to continue the armed struggle, and refused to lay down its arms. To confuse matters, one of the Army Council factions, using the new name Irish People's Liberation Army Organization killed an RUC Officer and also took a few shots at police stations.

The INLA Army Council, led by Steenson, issued a death list of 30 of the New GHQ faction. Killing began on 20 January 1986, when two New GHQ members, John O'Reilly and Thomas Power, were shot dead at a bar in Drogheda south of the Border. Reprisals followed; one victim was Mary McGlinchey, wife of the imprisoned Dominic who had been an active INLA member, and who was killed in Dundalk on 1 February. Another was Tony McClaskey, an informer, killed by the 'Army Council' faction for 'pin-pointing its members' to the New GHQ faction. Just inside the NI border, bodies of other victims were found, often gagged and bound.

On 15 March, Steenson was shot dead in an ambush in Belfast, shortly after a cease-fire had been agreed. Prominent Republicans and the RC clergy, appalled by this deadly feud that was discrediting the Republican image of unity and purpose, had been trying to end it. Steenson was the tenth victim. The Army Council took revenge, assassinating two more New GHQ men on 20th and 21st, bringing the roll of this INLA feud to twelve dead and eleven seriously wounded. Top INLA leaders then went into hiding from one another.

The Troubles Roll On Remorselessly

Elsewhere it was more of the same; in 1987, there had been increased violence in NI, with 93 terrorist-related deaths (as against 61 in 1986), of whom three were British Servicemen, sixteen RUC members and eight UDR Volunteers, bringing the total terrorist-related deaths in the Province from August 1969 to the end of 1987, to 2,618. There were also 600 shootings in 1987 (up from 385 in the previous year) and 226 explosions (up from 173).

The year 1988 had begun with a message from the Provisional IRA Army Council to all its members in prison or detention, stating that it intended to start the New Year 'defiantly and confidently'; added to it was another from Colonel Gaddafi of Libya, saying, 'I support the IRA morally and politically because it is a just cause.' In NI, the British Army began fitting anti-missile systems to its helicopters, in case any Soviet SAM-7 anti-aircraft missiles had got in to the hands of the PIRA in Bandit Country; in an under-cover operation the SAS discovered more than 100 rifles and thousands of rounds of ammunition in three cars driven by UDA members; and the tit-for-tat sectarian killing began again on 15 January.

A Popular Misconception The oft-repeated 'Swell of disgust and revulsion felt by the people everywhere', after each particularly nasty incident of terrorist carnage; sentiments echoed so fulsomely by politicians, and others, asserting that it will be to the detriment of the perpetrators, makes one wonder if this is really so, and if such platitudes are not just the words of wishful thinkers. Terrorists need an atmosphere of fear to gain their ultimate ends, humanitarian factors have no part in their make-up, or their programme; and they are little concerned with reprobation from their enemies. One feels that such terrorist carnage is deliberate, and planned to cause the maximum amount of death, injury and destruction, indiscriminate or otherwise. More can therefore be expected, as PIRA policy is to cause the British Government to turn away in 'disgust and revulsion', withdraw British troops, and 'let the Irish fight it out among themselves'.

The fact that the PIRA Army Council had promised not to repeat the Harrods bombing, and had said that the Enniskillen bombing had been a mistake, gave encouragement to those who fostered this misconception. They must have been disappointed at Lisburn, a staunchly Protestant town, and the Operational GHQ of the British Forces in NI, on the evening of 16 June 1988, after a Fun Run for Charity in which British soldiers took part. As the crowds were dispersing, a bomb affixed to a plain, unmarked vehicle, in which soldiers were travelling, exploded, killing six of them. The van happened to be in a side-street; had it exploded a few minutes earlier in the car-park, where an estimated 4,000 people were getting into their cars, the carnage would have been greater than that planned by the PIRA for Gibraltar. However, Gerry Adams must have thought the exploit was well worthwhile, when a father of one of the dead soldiers called on the Army to leave Ulster.

The Future? What of the future of the IRA? The political positions and aims of the protagonists have not changed, but have become more entrenched; the Border between NI and the ROI remains open; Bandit Country is virtually a No-Go area; and the British milirary presence remains, as this low-intensity conflict grinds remorselessly on.

There has been only one significant change, caused by the E*ksund* incident and the discovery of the SAM-7s that almost reached the PIRA. For a long time Irish governments have been watching the conflict complacently, waiting for the British to tire and quit. Maintenance of this attitude was dependant on the IRA being contained within reasonable bounds, i.e, as long as it did not threaten the security of the ROI and its existing system of government. The stated aim of the IRA to depose the Dublin Government was not taken seriously.

The probability of the IRA's obtaining SAM-7s and other sophisticated weaponry, together with the political activities and growing popular support of Sinn Fein, also set to contest elections in the ROI, shed a new light upon it. The Republican Movement had become dangerous and uncontrollable. This has resulted in slightly better, and more effective, but still reluctant, co-operation between Irish and British Security Forces, which will no doubt continue to develop until the IRA is cut down to size.

One can still foresee difficulties surfacing between the two governments over extradition and cross-Border co-operation in the future. Only recently at Port Laoise, in June 1988, an Irish judge rejected the British Government's application for the extradiction of Patrick McVeigh, a PIRA activist, wanted in Britain to answer charges of being involved in bombing incidents at Chelsea Barracks and in Oxford Street. In a seemingly perverse manner it was based on the technicality that McVeigh had not been formally identified in Court by a British Police Officer. Released from custody, McVeigh quickly disappeared underground. A British Police Officer had travelled to Port Laoise for this purpose, but had been told his identification evidence would not be necessary. This was the first British extradition application under a new agreement just worked out by the British and Irish Governments with this problem in mind, as on at least three occasions previously, extradition orders had been refused by Irish Courts on technicalities.

It is unlikely, however, that the Irish Government wants completely to crush the PIRA, as it keeps the international spot-light on the Northern Ireland Problem, and is a counter to the Loyalist para-military groups. It is also most unlikely that the PIRA will be easily crushed or eliminated, for as fast as one PIRA Volunteer is arrested, at least two more rush forward to take his place. PIRA strength has remained fairly constant during the last three years or so, being around the 600 activists mark, and Danny Morrison, most probably a PIRA Army Council member, stated in March 1988 that '200 Volunteers have been killed since 1970'. The PIRA has tremendous energy and enthusiasm, has strong and clever leadership, and is deeply dedicated to Republican ideals which it instills into the next generation. Legends have been and are being manufactured that will continue to inspire, and perhaps will never die. Despite setbacks, the PIRA is resilient, and the immediate future promises to be one of renewed violence, not only in NI, but also in England and the ROI.

Looking farther into the future, one feels that should the alternative British Government be returned to power, it would probable 'give away' Northern Ireland to the Irish Republic. That would be a recipe for civil war, in which NI would be *de facto* partitioned on sectarian battle-lines and the Hibernian island would, like the Ibernian Peninsula, contain two separate nations – a lot of blood would be spilt in the process.

5. The Basque ETA

This Etarra, as active ETA gunmen are known, is posing for journalists at a press conference being held by the organization. He is masked to conceal his identity from both the Spanish security forces and more sinister groups which track down and execute suspected ETA members.

'Yoyes: *Death to a Traitor*' – Graffito about a repentant ETA Member who accepted 'Social Integration'.

ON 25 August 1987, Filipe Gonzales, the Spanish Prime Minister, declared that the greatest problem facing his country was that of Terrorism, and while boasting that its back had been broken by his Security Forces, he emphasized that vigilance was still necessary to crush it.

Spain was plagued by two major terrorist organizations and several minor ones; Groupo de Resistancia Antifascista Primero de Octubre (GRAPO), meaning the '1st October Anti-Fascist Group', had emerged in 1976 after Franco's death, as the militant wing of the re-constituted Spanish Communist Party. GRAPO carried out terrorist activity against right-wing and alleged Fascist targets; it was separate from ETA, with no connections of any signficance at all, and therefore does not form part of this study.

The 'Euskadi Ta Askentasvna' (ETA), is usually translated as 'Basque Homeland and Liberty'. They began a campaign of violence in pursuit of Basque Independence in 1968, and since then have been responsible for more than 500 terrorist-related deaths. In 1980 more than 400 of its terrorists were in Spanish gaols; their motivation stems from a combination of nationalism and radicalism.

The Basques

The larger part of ethnic Basque territory (South Euskadi) is located in the northern-most part of Spain, and comprises the three Provinces of Viscaya, Guipuzcoa and Alava, each having a huge Basque majority, and Navarra Province, in which the smaller Basque majority is debatable. Across the frontier in the south-western corner of France, are the three Basque Provinces of Labourd, Soule and Lower Navarre (North Euskadi). There are probably 2.7 million Basques in Spain, and about 300,000 in France; varying estimates being coloured by political prejudices. Spanish Basque territory includes the cities of Vitoria (regional capital), Bilbao (industrial and with a probable population of 450,000), Guernica, Pamplona and San Sebastian.

The Basques have an ancient culture, language and history, and have been mainly hill farmers and fishermen, their way of life changing little over the centuries. They tend to be insular and nationalistic in character. Spanish Basques backed the wrong side in the Second Carlist War of 1876 and lost many of their ancient privileges as a result, while the French Basques lost theirs in the French Revolution of 1789.

While Spanish Basques are generally robust, energetic and politically active, French Basques tend to be more placid and conservative, more interested in language and culture than in the armed struggle. There was just one small terrorist group in French Basque territory, known as the 'Iparretarrak' or Men from the North. Formed in 1972, it had little local support, and none at all from ETA.

During the Spanish Civil War (1936–9) the Basques, who had just been granted a limited form of autonomy by the Spanish Republican Government, fought on its side against Franco's Nationalists. As the victor, General Franco unified Spain by force, acting harshly against any form of separatism. The Basque Flag (Ikorpina), almost a sacred symbol, language and customs were banned.

Euskadi Ta Askentasvna – ETA

Euskadi Ta Askentasvna (ETA) was formed in July 1959, by a group of young student activists who broke away from the turgid Basque Nationalist Party (PNV), founded in 1895. ETA's purpose was to fight the Franco regime, and ultimately to gain Basque Independence. Development was slow, and it was not until 2 August 1968, that ETA carried out its first major terrorist operation, the assassination of the Chief of Police at San Sebastian, which led to the much-publicized 'Burgos-17 Trial', when death sentences were pronounced. It took years to recover from this, but when it re-emerged it did so in spectacular fashion when the 'Trikis Brigade' assassinated the Spanish Prime Minister, Admiral Luis Carrero, in December 1973.

Franco died in December 1975 ushering in a new era in Spain's history. A Spanish Democratic Constitution was approved in 1978, and a Referendum held in Basque territory in 1979 decided in favour of autonomy. The Statute of Guernica provided for an 'Autonomous Basque Community within the Spanish State', to be called 'Euskadi'. On 11 January 1980, the three Basque Provinces (Navarra was not included) became an 'Autonomous Region of Spain'. Elections were held in March, for the Vitoria-based Basque Regional Assembly, and the Basque flag, language and customs were again freely permitted.

With such a degree of autonomy achieved, what reason did ETA have to continue with the armed struggle? This was a question ETA asked itself. After the death of Franco and the dawning of a new democratic era in Spain, differences arose within ETA as to which course to pursue. One faction, which wanted to give Spanish democracy a chance, and to concentrate only upon political activity, emerged in 1977, and became known as the ETA-Politico-Militar' (ETA-PM), or the 'Poli-Milis', which renounced violence except in self-defence. The other faction decided to continue the armed struggle for independence, and became known as 'ETA-Militar' (ETA-M).

ETA Organization Both factions were controlled by their respective Executive Committees, the Chairman of which, being the leader and senior executive, was usually known as the Chief of Staff. Most Executive Committee members had certain individual responsibilities, such as for Intelligence, Operations. Logistics, and so on similar to the IRA model. Active members were formed into small teams, or commandos, each of up to a dozen or so individuals; the remainder being employed in less exacting tasks. Secrecy was good within ETA (an expression used to include all factions) and neither Spanish nor French Security Forces were ever really certain which Top Terrorist did which Top Job. A variety of aliases and code-names were adopted by leaders and activists, some of whom had two or more. In 1980, the leader of the ETA-M was Domingo Iturbi Abesolo, code-named 'Txomin'; while the leader of the ETA-PM was probably Joseba Aulesia, alias 'Zotza'. Leaders, Executive Committee members and activists were invariably long-serving ETA veterans; they came in two categories, the 'Legales' living in Spain, and the 'Liberados', living outside Spain, mainly in France. By 1980, the two ETA factions had parted company completely, and indeed occasionally scuffled with each other.

Both groups had their own political wings, or 'fronts'; that of the Poli-Milis being the 'Euskadiko Eskerra' (EE), meaning Basque Left, which was legalized in 1978; while that of the ETA-M was the 'Herri Batasuna' (HB), meaning 'People's Unity', still not fully legalized, but tolerated by the authorities. ETA-PM tended to favour a Marxist-Leninist platform, but ETA-M was hostile to Communism because of its gradualist approach to revolution.

When Basque autonomy was achieved, both factions decided to continue the struggle for independence against the central government; ETA-M with active terrorism, as its leadership believed the best course was to provoke the Government into declaring Martial Law, which would repress the Basques, who then might be persuaded to rise in mass rebellion. Dissatisfied with the limited powers accorded to the Basque Regional Assembly, and by the exclusion of Navarra Province, the Poli-Milis decided to continue the political struggle.

Strength In 1980, according to the *Policia Espanol*, a police magazine, ETA had about 600 activists in Spain, 200 in France, 100 in Belgium, and another 100 in Venezuela. ETA terrorists had received training in South Yemen, Lebanon, Ireland, Uruguay and Cuba; while the Soviet Union, China and Libya had provided some economic support. General police estimates were that ETA probably numbered more than 3,000. Not all were active terrorists; many merely formed part of the essential back-up support; to which should be added an additional unknown number of sympathizers, active and passive. Such figures were only selective estimates, which varied depending upon who was using them, and for what purpose. As the popularity of ETA declined with the catalyst of Franco removed from the scene, so did its number of helpers and sympathizers.

Training Owing to an initial lack of expertise, ETA suffered several self-inflicted deaths and injuries due to premature bomb explosions. In one incident in Vitoria early in 1983, a premature explosion killed two terrorists; and a few days later two more were killed by their own bomb which they were priming to explode near a bank. In August that year, two more ETA terrorists were killed by an explosion in San

Sebastian. Similar incidents continued to occur periodically and in the mid 1980s, ETA-M persuaded the Provisional IRA to send one of its top bomb-makers from Ireland, to help improve expertise in this deadly art.

Funding ETA raised money by intimidating local communities into paying protection money, and other forms of extortion. They also levied 'Revolutionary Taxes' on banks, industrial and commercial firms, and individuals, thought able to pay them. At first only small amounts were demanded, and usually paid, but these were soon followed by letters demanding larger, regular contributions, accompanied by the latest bank statement of the firm or individual. Failure to pay Revolutionary Taxes resulted in damage to property, usually by explosions, threats to individuals, and for persistent non-payment, injury or assassination. Often wealthy individuals were kidnapped, and a large ransom was demanded, in addition to resumption of payment of Revolutionary Taxes. Sometimes money was lodged in banks in French Basque territory, to avoid the ever-present Government threat of sequestration.

Saturnino Orbegoza, an industrialist who refused to pay his Revolutionary Taxes, was seized by the Poli-Milis, in November 1982 when leaving church. A ransom of the equivalant of US $800,000 was demanded, but Zotza, the ETA-PM leader, said he was willing trade his hostage for the release of 74 ETA-PM terrorists held in prison. After 46 days in captivity, a Civil Guard anti-terrorist team, stormed a cottage north of Pamplona, where Orbegoza was being held, and rescued him. This was yet another police success and banks in the Spanish Basque Region decided to resist paying Revolutionary Taxes. The ETA reply came quickly when an explosion at the Bank of Viscayo, in Bilbao, killed two people and injured others; it is believed that bank payments to ETA were then resumed. However the incident sparked a massive Basque demonstration in protest against ETA terrorist activities, in which all Basque political parties participated except the HB.

Tactics and Activities Intitially, ETA had planned to disrupt the prosperous Spanish tourist industry in order to damage the Spanish economy; and in 1979, explosions at the airport and two railway stations in Madrid, had killed seven people and injured more than 120, but neither tourists nor foreigners were among the casualties. Each year ETA-M ran an anti-tourist campaign, causing a few explosions, usually at night, at main holiday resorts, with the object of alarming, rather than killing or maiming tourists. For example, during 1985, only nineteen small explosions were recorded; but the following year more than 8,000 extra police had to be deployed in Spanish Mediterranean resorts, which was a big drain on security manpower. This pattern of small explosions with few, if any, casualties at holiday resorts continued. The Spanish tourist industry claimed that it was only marginally affected. In May 1985 a car-bomb, parked near a hotel in Torremolinos on the Costa del Sol, and undiscovered for more than a month, was found by accident and defuzed.

ETA-Militar During 1980, 85 (of the 128) terrorist-related deaths recorded in Spain were considered by the security authorities to have been committed by ETA-M. In January that year the Chief of Police of Alava Province was shot dead when travelling in his car to his office; a typical ETA target although Alava and Navarra Provinces were unique, as even under the Franco regime they had managed to retain a local police force. While escorting a munitions truck in February, civil guards ran into an ambush, and six of them were killed by ETA. A couple of years later two ETA-M terrorists, Angel Maria Recalde and Fancisco Maria Esquiva were convicted of this crime, and another perpetrator, Tomas Linaza Echevarria escaped to France.

A funeral service of an ETA terrorist who had been 'killed in action' by the police, was held at Durango, near Bilbao, in the same month. When the priest conducting the service condemned Basque violence, he was shouted down by a particularly large congregation of mourners, who continually chanted 'Gora ETA-Militar' (Long live ETA-M), as the priest indignantly walked out of the church. On the same day, at another funeral service for an ETA terrorist, who had been gunned down by the Spanish Basque Battalion (BVE), an anti-ETA formation, mourners turned the occasion into a political demonstration, singing their 'Eusko Gudariak' (Soldier's Song). This gave an indication of the depths of general support for ETA, a hang-over from the days when it opposed the Franco regime.

In March, near San Sebastian, a 13-year-old boy was killed and his 12-year-old companion lost his sight when an ETA bomb attached to a policeman's car exploded; the policeman had decided to walk to work that day. This was the 32nd terrorist-related death that year. Other typical incidents included the ambushing and killing of an army officer, and the shooting dead of three Civil Guards in a café in San Sebastian (in May 1980); and the stealing of eight-tons of 'Goma-2' explosives by eight terrorists in Civil Guard uniforms. In June a female anti-terrorist squad member was killed besieging a house where ETA members were hiding; picked more or less at random, these incidents illustrate the pattern of terrorism that had become commonplace in the Basque region. During the whole of 1980, eight ETA terrorists were shot dead by Civil Guards, while fourteen Civil Guards had been killed by ETA terrorists.

ETA-Politics Although temporarily foreswearing violence the Poli-Milis indulged in kidnapping for money and publicity. In January 1981 the ETA-PM kidnapped Luis Suner, reputedly the richest man in Spain (declarable taxable income was then published in the media), and at 71 was the oldest such victim so far. He was held for 90 days, and then quietly released unharmed, it being presumed that a large ransom had been paid. Security Forces tried to block ransom payments, and indeed in a previous kidnap situation, Poli-Milis had been foiled by a police trap, which this time they had managed to evade.

The following month, the Poli-Milis kidnapped the Consuls of El Salvador and Austria in Bilbao, and of Uruguay in Pamplona; but failed to seize two more who did not go to their offices that morning. ETA-PM demanded in return for their safe release the publication in full, in the media, of Amnesty International's Report on brutality by Spanish Security Forces, and also of photographs of the body of a suspected terrorist, who had allegedly died of torture while in police custody. This incident led to the introduction of legislation forbidding the media to publish any such terrorist material in future.

The Cortes Incident: February 1981

Suddenly, on 23 February 1981, a most dramatic incident occurred. It was depicted on world television screens as cameramen were on the spot, in the Spanish Cortes (Parliament), when Lieutenant Colonel Antonio Tejero de Molino, of the Civil Guards, entered, drew his pistol and fired shots into the ceiling. Tejero and his Civil Guards took over the Cortes while Deputies cowered behind desks and seats. Swift action by King Juan Carlos in summoning leaders of political parties for consultation, defuzed the situation and thwarted a military rebellion.

Government Reaction The Spanish Government was severely shaken by the attempted military *coup*, and as soon as Calvo Sotelo was confirmed as Prime Minister in a new civilian government, he decided to clamp down on terrorism, and limit Basque autonomy. On 23 March 1981, he established the 'Unified Anti-Terrorist Command' (UATC), under the Minister of the Interior, which included military commanders of regions, military and civil intelligence agencies, the Civil Guard, the national police, and certain other individuals. The Spanish Security Forces had certainly been unprepared for combined operations against terrorists; and for example, hardly anyone in them could speak Basque, and so all had to rely upon Basque interpreters, who were instinctively hostile. The same day, the Prime Minister ordered the Army to enter the fight against terrorism; and one of its first tasks was to seal off the open French border. Before long, Army patrols were handicapping the former free-ranging cross-border movement of ETA.

The changes revitalized the Security Forces and they now went on to the offensive; by the end of its first operational year, UATC had arrested 1,260 suspected terrorists, and recovered more than 600 illegal weapons. An improved intelligence picture led to the conclusion that each ETA group had a number of small commando teams in the Basque provinces, others that operated in Madrid, Barcelona and the main cities, and a number of 'roving' teams outside the Basque region. Their first big capture on 14 June 1981 was of two top ETA-men, named as José Luis Polguer and Urreta Viscaya.

UATC's military capabilities were impressive too; when Doctor Julio Iglesias was kidnapped in Madrid by ETA-PM in December 1981, and a huge ransom demanded for his release, he was rescued by a UATC team, which stormed a country house in a mountain village near Saragossa, to capture four sleeping terrorists. This was the first ETA-PM incident since its cease-fire declaration, it being excused owing to 'the permanent need for funds'. This rescue boosted the reputation of the UATC and the morale of the Security Forces generally. As a follow-up, the UATC discovered a large Poli-Milis arms cache, which included rocket-launchers and machine-guns, in a house near Bilbao. It is believed the information came from one of the captured terrorists, who had been guarding Doctor Iglesias.

ETA Reaction The Tejero attempt to disrupt democratic government alarmed the leadership of the Poli-Milis, which realized that if a military government came to power, all political gains made by the Basques would be swept away. Zotza quickly called a secret press conference on 1 March; invited journalists were blind-folded, taken in a truck to a country house, where a hooded Zotza flanked by hooded lieutenants, announced that ETA-PM would 'call off its armed struggle without any conditions'. The same day the three Consuls seized earlier were released.

On the other hand, ETA-M, led by Txomin, remained steadfastly intent on destabilizing the democratic government and hastening the revolution; and he rejected the idea of a cease-fire. Txomin said his group would continue with the armed struggle, and concentrate upon assassinating senior officers. A police colonel was killed in March; then a colonel in Pamplona, and another in Bilbao. In April, another colonel was shot dead in San Sebastian, and a Civil Guard colonel in Bilbao, when buying a newspaper, by a young girl who from her description, had killed an army officer in the same city some two months previously. Another colonel was shot dead leaving church in June, and yet another was wounded in Irun when leaving a cinema. The assassins all used 9mm Parabellum weapons.

Counter-Insurgency and the Dirty War

The Security Forces Strictly speaking the Civil Guard, conspicious with its curious tricorn hat with turned-up rear brim, and formal 19th-century military uniform, was charged with a counter-insurgency responsibility against ETA, and other terrorist groups. This para-military force, more than 50,000 strong, was commanded by regular army officers, while the men were recruited from the poorer regions of Spain after completing military conscript service. Civil Guards were a self-contained community, living in barracks with their families and largely cut off from the people. The Commandant of the Civil Guards, General José Saens de Sabtmaria, objected to the employment of the army against terrorists and, quoting the British experience in Ulster, said in 1981, 'Let us be realistic. Against whom are we to deploy the army? Comparison with Britain is eloquent enough. The real problem is to isolate terrorists from the rest of the community.'

The National Police, almost 60,000 strong, was the normal civilian police force, although the men were armed, deployed in cities and towns, and commanded by regular army officers. Partly as a result of their success – which was severely undermining ETA – and to ensure its continuation, Rafael Vera, Chief of UATC, announced the launch of Operation 'Zen' (Zone Español del Norte) in May 1983 to boost their performance even further. Pay, conditions of service, and special allowances for serving in the Basque region were to be improved; psychological training was to be given to improve relations between the Security Forces and the Basque people; and modern equipment and expertise were to be acquired. Operation 'Zen' upset the Basque Regional Assembly, which had not been consulted beforehand, because the Basque Regional Police were not included.

The wave of anti-terrorist measures were compounded in September 1984 by legislation that allowed the police to hold a suspect for ten days instead of four without charging him, and to close newspapers if they praised terrorists, apologized for their actions, or published any of their communiqués or demands.

The Uncontrollables ETA activists tended to live on the French side of the frontier, cross it to commit a terrorist crime in Spain, and then quickly return to their sanctuary. When flushed out by Spanish Security Forces, ETA terrorists, if they could, also fled across the border into France along one of the numerous mountain tracks across the Pyrenees. Spanish Security Forces had to stop short at the frontier; the French authorities ignored their problem, and cynically refused to co-operate in any way. For years relations between French and Spanish governments had ranged from abrasive to ice-cold. This frustration gave rise to groups of anti-ETA 'Uncontrollables', who crossed into France to take a covert war into the ETA sanctuary. These included the 'Armed Spanish Group' (GAE); the 'Anti-Communist Alliance' (Triple A); and the 'Spanish Basque Battalion', (BVE). In the late 1970s and early 1980s, these groups consisted of hired thugs and gunmen with dubious backgrounds. No one would admit responsibility for them, although suspicion pointed to Spanish Government intelligence agencies; but nothing could be proved. Jesus Garcia, named in the Spanish media as the organizer of the Uncontrollables, was shot dead in San Sebastian in January 1980 by ETA gunmen.

That month, a bomb placed in a bar in Bilbao, frequented by ETA members, exploded killing four people and injuring nineteen others. Towards the end of the year, three members of the BVE crossed into the French border town of Hendaye, fired their automatic weapons into a café known to be an ETA haunt, killing two and wounding ten others, then sped back again, crashing through the frontier barrier, to be arrested on Spanish soil. A senior police officer in Madrid, Manuel Ballisteros, ordered their instant release, but later refused to identify them, claiming they were paid informers. Ballisteros was later charged with withholding information, and his case dragged on through the Courts, until he was finally acquitted by the Supreme Court in March 1986, his act being justified because he was 'the confidant of mercenaries in the anti-terrorist struggle'. This decision appeared to give such activities official approval and served to encourage their continuance.

Within a period of two years, five senior ETA leaders had been killed while on the run in France, including José Martin Gagardia, victim of a car-bomb in Biarritz; and Miguel Antonio Glokoetxes alias 'Txapela', one of their top gunmen, himself shot in an ambush at St Jean de Luz in 1983. Innocent people too were occasionally caught in the crossfire of this war.

The Barrios Incident In October 1983, Captain Alberto Barrios was kidnapped in Bilbao by the ETA-M and the release of eight 'Etarras' (ETA members or suspects) charged with armed robbery, was demanded in exchange for his safe release. A demand was also made for full publication in the media of an ETA-M account of the incident. Only the radio, in response to a special plea from the Captain's family, risked prosecution by giving a short summarized extract: but it was too late. A fortnight later Captain Barrios's body was found. He was the 37th military officer to be killed by terrorists since 1977, and the 38th person that year. The nation registered its protest against Basque terrorism by one-minute's silence in cities when all traffic stopped. Even the HB condemned this murder as a 'political blunder'.

The GAL Four The day after the Captain's body was found, four members of the Anti-Terrorist Liberation Group (GAL), reputedly led by Ishmael Miguel Gutilpez, entered French Basque territory, went into a bar and shot dead Ramon Oneaderra alias 'Kutu', a notorious ETA-M leader. The following day this GAL team tried to kidnap Txomin, who had just been released from prison. They rammed his motor cycle, seized him and tried to force him into their car. Passing police intervened in time to save him and the four GAL activists were arrested. Two other top ETA-M leaders disappeared at about this time and have not been seen again; presumably they were murdered by these shady anti-Basque death squads.

Little or nothing was known about GAL, which had mysteriously appeared, seemingly to supersede the previous collection of mercenary anti-ETA groups, known as the Uncontrollables. Suspicion pointed to the recently established UATC. It was assumed that the shadowy organization was financed by bankers, businessmen and industrialists; tired of paying Revolutionary Taxes they had hired contract killers for 'special tasks'. In Hendaye a French businessman was kidnapped by GAL, who offered to release him for the four GAL members detained in French custody. Alarmed by the 'dirty war' that was developing on French soil, the Gal four were hastily released for lack of evidence.

The dirty war continued apace during 1984, and among the Basques them-selves. Tomas Linaza Echevarria, a veteran founder-member of ETA, wanted by the

Spanish police for involvement in the killing of the six Civil Guards in 1980, and other assassinations, was fatally wounded in June when his motor cycle was booby-trapped; GAL claimed responsibility. 'Anton le Grand' (Antonio Pego), reputed leader of the Anti-Capitalist Autonomous Command (CAA), an ETA splinter group, was killed by GAL near San Sebastian in August. He had been responsible for the assassination of Senator Enrique Casa, a Basque politican, during the recent regional elections; the act having been claimed by the 'Menedku' (Vengeance) Group, the political front for the CAA.

Doctor Santiago Brouard, leader and founder-member of the HB, was shot dead in Bilbao in November, by hooded gunmen who forced their way into his house. GAL claimed responsibility for its first assassination on Spanish soil. The following day, the Spanish Commando shot and wounded General Luis Rosen, in a Madrid street. In this tit-for-tat assassination competition the police gave the tally as GAL thirteen and ETA twenty-two.

GAL remained active in 1985; in March they assassinated Francisco Galdeano Araha, founder of the Basque language newspaper, *Ergin*; and in September four GAL activists entered a café in Bayonne, and shot dead four ETA terrorists. Owing to lack of positive information, coupled with many wild rumours, it was frequently alleged that GAL was not a real organization as such, but underworld mercenaries hired for particular jobs.

The Spanish Commandos

Madrid Commando The ETA-M Spanish Commando, led by 'Maserio', Ignacio Aracama, had been active in Madrid since 1978, and indeed was often referred to as the 'Madrid Commando'. It consisted of about a dozen activists, with ample back-up support, and its targets in the first part of the 1980s were mainly military officers, some twenty such attacks having been made. But the Spanish Commando carried out other types of terrorist acts.

One occurred in April 1982, when bombs exploded in the main telephone exchange in Madrid, severing overseas communication links, and causing considerable internal disruption. Terrorists had gained entry by wearing Civil Guard uniforms. After this incident, the Army was brought in to guard telephone installations.

Another took place in March the following year, when Diego Oardo Colon, a banker, and direct descendant of Christopher Colombus, was kidnapped by four members of the Spanish Commando, posing as policemen. He was a personal friend of the King, and special efforts were made to find and rescue him, including several intensive searches of parts of Madrid, but without success. Diego Colon was quietly released after 73 days in captivity, it being presumed that a large ransom had been paid. This made the Government concentrate its mind on anti-ransom legislation.

Several years later, in 1986, another descendant of Christopher Columbus, Admiral Cristobal Colon, was killed in Madrid by the ETA-M Spanish Commando. His car was boxed-in on a narrow street, one terrorist threw a grenade into the car, and the other fired his 9mm Parabellum at the victim. The choice of these two victims was obviously influenced by their famous ancestor, known to every schoolchild the world over, and so international publicity was gained by ETA-M.

The killing of senior military officers continued; early in 1984 Spanish Commando gunmen shot and killed General Guillermo Quintana, as he was walking home from church. According to the police he was killed with, 'lethal professionalism'. This prompted the Minister of the Interior to state that '6,000 police in Madrid are on full-time protection duties guarding Government ministers and senior military officers.'

During 1985, the Spanish Commando began placing car-bombs along routes used by military and Civil Guard convoys, and in September, during the Madrid morning rush-hour, a remote-controlled car-bomb was detonated as a bus carrying Civil Guards was passing, injuring sixteen of them and two civilians. In April the following year, another car-bomb exploded as a Land Rover carrying Civil Guards passed by (a carbon copy of the previous incident), killing five of them and injuring another four, as well as two civilians. In June, two men and a woman of the Spanish Commando ambushed an army car, killing two officers and the driver. During 1986, the Spanish Commando was responsible for 22 deaths in Madrid.

A breakthrough came that July with the arrest of three members of the Spanish Commando, named as Ines del Rio Prada, Angel Luis Hermosa, and Jean-Philippe Casabonne, a French Basque. Information gained from them by the police enabled photographs of four more wanted terrorists to be issued, whom they believed were hiding in safe-houses in Madrid. A bugged car led the Security Forces to an apartment in Madrid, where six members, three men and three women, of the Spanish Commando were arrested. The Police stated that only the leader, Maserio, and two other top accomplices were still at large. This considerably lessened the spate of terrorism carried out by the Spanish Commando, which in ten years had been responsible for more than 60 deaths; except for one small sting in the tail, when in May, three car-bombs exploded in Madrid, killing one person and injuring others. This suggested that a new unit might have been established.

The Barcelona Commando In the latter part of the decade the ETA-M Barcelona Commando became active, in the city that was bidding to become the location for the 1992 World Olympic Games. Three car-bombs exploded in Barcelona in March 1987, killing a Civil Guard, and injuring fifteen people, and in June, another bomb exploded at a supermarket, the seventh since October 1986, which killed seventeen people and injured 31, many being burned by inflammable liquid.

Political Offensives

The Seventh Assembly: ETA-PM Although the Poli-Milis virtually ended their cease-fire when their members made a bazooka attack on a Civil Guard building, in February 1982, discussion within the leadership continued as to whether to do so officially. This led, in September, to its Seventh Assembly being summoned, in secret on French territory. The previous ETA-PM Assembly (the Sixth) had been in 1976; at the Seventh Assembly, Juan Maria Bandres, leader of the EE Party, the political front for ETA-PM, said he had already been negotiating secretly with the Government for an amnesty for ETA prisoners, in return for abandoning violence. Previously, in April, the HB, the political front for the ETA-M, had tried to open secret negotiations on similar lines, but had been rebuffed.

Ten prominent ETA-PM members, who became known as the 'Seventh Assembly' Group, held a secret press conference, on 30 September, somewhere in

France, to announce that it had decided to renounce violence, would dissolve itself, and welcomed the new Socialist Government of Filipe Gonzales, due to take office in December. This time Zotza, and his lieutenants, appeared before the Press without hoods, and one, Miren Lourdes Alcorta, solemnly read out the announcement. The Government released 22 (of the 74 held) Poli-Milis members from prison.

The Eighth Assembly The rump of the Poli-Milis met as the 'Eighth Assembly' in October, and issued a statement in the name of their leader, Inakil Elorriaga, who was in prison, saying that his faction, which became known as the 'ETA-PM (VIII)', or the 'Octavos', would observe a 100 days' truce, to give the Socialist Government a chance to show how it proposed to handle Basque affairs. Three ETA factions now existed: ETA-M; ETA-PM (VII); and ETA-PM (VIII). All wanted an independent Basque Republic that included French Basque territory, but all approached the problem in a different way. ETA-PM (VII) did not dissolve itself, but remained militarily inactive.

Government Hearts and Minds The 'Battle for the Allegiance of the Basque People' campaign was launched in the Cortes in November 1983, the Government insisting that it would not negotiate with terrorists, which it was already secretly doing. While making it an offence to be a 'go-between', the Government did not go as far as to authorize the prosecution of those who paid ransoms, although one industrialist had been briefly detained by the police for negotiating with his captors. The Government also hesitated to freeze funds held in banks to prevent ransoms being paid.

Anxious to show its good democratic character, because it was angling for membership of the European Economic Community (EEC) in July, it clarified telephone-tapping regulations, permitting them only if authorized by a magistrate under the Anti-Terrorist Act, or at the request of someone being threatened by terrorists. Also, to ensure that justice was being seen to be done, three Civil Guards were convicted of involvement in the deaths of three innocent civilians in 1980.

French Co-operation The open French border, and French attitude were considerable handicaps to the Spanish Government in its fight against terrorism. This dated from the Spanish Civil War, when the French had backed the losing Republican side; after which they gave a special status to Spanish refugees, especially Basques, fleeing from the Franco regime. When Spain returned to democracy, France, still cherishing its high reputation for granting political asylum, remained reluctant to co-operate with Spain on anti-terrorist measures. Indeed, as late as 1981, the French Minister of the Interior was reported to have remarked that the 'ETA struggle is like that of the French Resistance during the war'.

Largely due to the continuing dirty war being waged on their Basque territory between the Uncontrollables and ETA, the French police stirred themselves and made a few arrests in 1982. In June, Txomin, leader of ETA-M, was picked up and given a short prison sentence for illegal possession of a firearm. Two other important arrests, followed in November: 'Paio el Viajo' alias Luis Antony Larrangage, ETA-M's Director of Intelligence and deputy leader; also the Director of Finance, Carlos Ibargurren otherwise known as 'Nevios' who was responsible for collecting Revolutionary Taxes. Information gained from these and other arrests led the French police to several caches of arms, ammunition and explosives. Also found were lists of more than 90 'subscribers' of Revolutionary Taxes, the methods of collection, penalties for non-payment and boxes of false identity documents. It all amounted to a considerable haul, dealing another blow to the organization.

The first big security sweep proper in French Basque territory began in January 1984, when police raided the homes of 100 known ETA terrorists, intending to arrest about 50 of them, but only managing to catch twelve; the remainder, having been warned by sympathizers, had hastily decamped. As agreed with the Spanish Government, the French deported six of them to a 'third country', and the others to enforced residence in northern France. Other arrests, with similar results, followed. This was a great shock to ETA's complacency as its French sanctuary began to crumble away; worse was to come.

In August, the Spanish Minister of the Interior openly complained that during the previous eighteen months not a single one of his 106 applications to France for the extradition of ETA terrorists had been granted. However, a start had been made in June when an agreement on this issue was reached between the two countries. On the 10th, a French Court ruled that four ETA terrorists should be extradited to Spain; on the 16th, the French withdrew their Special Status for Spanish refugees; and on the 30th, in another security sweep, more than 30 ETA suspects were detained. This caused a minor back-lash of damage to French property and cars. That month Belgium extradited two ETA terrorists to Spain; and in September, France finally began to do the same.

French security sweeps continued spasmodically in Basque territory during 1985; two top activists, named as Juan Lorenza Lasa and Felix Zabarde, were detained, as were others of lesser importance. These arrests decimated the leadership of ETA-M, and the surviving members of the Executive Committee drew themselves into a smaller, tighter directorate of four or five members, for security.

Negotiations In March 1984 Txomin, leader of ETA-M, began secret negotiations with the Spanish Government via the Basque Regional Government, and the French Embassy in Madrid. Thinking ETA terrorists were becoming weary and were psychologically ready for a cease-fire, the Government demanded that they lay down their arms, and that exiles become 'socially integrated'. Txomin, on the other hand, thought the Government was tired of the insurgency and, wanting to end it, would grant considerable concessions. Txomin stuck rigidly to the 'KAS Alternatives' of 1977, and would not budge; neither would the Government. Both had misjudged the other. The KAS (Basque Socialist Support) group conditions had included self-determination for the Basques, withdrawal of the Civil Guard, Basque control of military formations in the region, and a general amnesty.

The Ertzantza In March 1985 Carlos Diaz Arkoche, Chief of the Basque Regional Police, the 'Ertzantza', was killed by a car-bomb explosion when he switched on the ignition of his car. He had invariably followed the same routine daily, and so was a sitting duck. GAL was an obvious suspect, but ETA tended to blame 'government agents'. It was most probably ETA-M terrorists who wanted to stop the development of the Ertzantza, and its acceptance by the Basque people which, it was planned, was eventually to take the place of both the Civil Guard and National Police, whose presence irritated Basques.

Distinguishable in red berets, the first batch of Basque policemen had graduated from the new Police College at Vitoria in February 1983, and further graduates had brought the force up to a strength of about 3,000; its establishment having been set at about the 7,000 mark. It had an unfortunate start, as on the eve of its first day on the streets, ETA terrorists raided a police station in San Sebastian, disarmed ten new Basque policemen, tied them up, and escaped in a police Land Rover with more than 100 new firearms, ammunition and police uniforms. Since then the central government has blown hot and cold on the Ertzantza, which the Basques themselves still hesitate to accept.

Repentance and Clemency Taking a leaf from the Italian Security Forces' book, the Spanish Government instituted what amounted to a dual 'Repentance and Clemency' programme, and a supergrass system, both to undermine the ETA leadership by syphoning away manpower, and to obtain information. Telephone numbers to contact in confidence were boldly displayed. This scheme was also available to ETA terrorists in prison, although those convicted of capital crimes were excluded, at least in theory. The offer to terrorists to come in out of the cold was based on psychology, and the dreariness and weariness of the long haul, aimed at veteran ETA terrorists, now in middle age, many of whom wanted more personal comforts, and perhaps to marry and settle down, instead of continually looking over their shoulder. This dual approach drove the ETA leadership farther underground, forcing it to take extra security precautions, and increased the difficulty of keeping in touch with its scattered members.

A notable 'repentant' was Zotza, leader of the moribund ETA-PM (VII), who had married his lieutenant, Miren Lourdes Alcorta (who had read out the Declaration of Dissolution to the Press), and who persuaded most of his supporters to accept the Government's 'Social Integration' programme; he later claimed, in January 1985, that he was the last of his 144-strong ETA-PM (VII) membership to be accepted.

More tragic was the veteran woman ETA-M Executive Committee member, and long-time activist, 'Yoyes', Maria Dolores Gonzales, who, having a two-year-old son, wanted to opt out from terrorism and live a normal life. She obtained Txomin's permission to do so, and in 1985, returned to her small home town of Ordizoa near San Sebastian to be greeted by graffiti reading 'Yoyes: Death to a Traitor.' Txomin had promised her his protection, and although she was ostracized, she was left alone. Her peaceful new existence was to be violently shattered.

Meanwhile, the supergrass system was instrumental in locating terrorists' caches of arms, but was less successful in obtaining witnesses for the prosecution. In one case, however, information came from an entirely different source – from the owner of a garage where ETA arms were stored, whose wife ran away with an ETA terrorist. Before he committed suicide, the embittered man passed on information in detail to the police, including how to defuse the booby-trap protecting the cache.

Civil Guard: Demilitarization The Civil Guard was slowly acquiring expertise in its war against the ETA terrorists, but was hampered by its rigid military form and attitude. It had its successes and failures. In February 1984, a Civil Guard anti-terrorist team ambushed a dinghy, carrying five CAA terrorists on a kidnapping mission, at the port of Paseajes, killing four of them and capturing the fifth. This led to the formation of a Civil Guard coastal amphibious section to counter terrorism and drug smuggling. Some frogmen were trained, as it was suspected ETA was acquiring expertise for exploding underwater bombs. However, in September, three Civil Guards were killed and five wounded when they walked into an ambush on a railway embankment near Vitoria. A nigh invisible nylon fishing-line had been used as the trip-wire.

Certain reforms were introduced into the Civil Guard with the object of demilitarizing it, and also into the National Police, but they made slow progress for some time due to a degree of internal resistance. In 1985, civilians were appointed to Head both the Civil Guard and the National Police, and to further advance the demilitarization programme.

Operation 'Clam' In the mid-1980s, both the French Direction Générale de la Sécurité Etranges (DGSE) (Overseas Intelligence Service), and the American Central Intelligence Agency (CIA) collaborated with the Spanish police, and introduced certain sophisticated equipment, which included electronic 'bugs'. During 1985, in Operation 'Clam', arms and vehicles with electronic bugs attached were allowed to fall into terrorist hands, which enabled several of them to be tracked and arrested, and arms caches to be located. In one case bugs affixed to two rocket-launchers, led French police to a furniture factory with a huge underground arsenal at St-Pée-sur-Nivelle, about seven miles from the Spanish border. The police collected three truck-loads of arms and ammunition, and boxes of incriminating documents.

While searching for a Basque wanted for murder, in September 1987, the French police closed in on an isolated farmhouse at Anglet, near Bayonne, and found 'Santi Potros', or Santiago Lasa, then ETA-M Director of Operations, together with a gold-mine of incriminating documents that listed more than 600 ETA-M members, locations of arms caches, safe-houses, and a 'people's prison'. Also found at the farmhouse were two ready-rigged car-bombs, stolen vehicles, arms, explosives, and electronic apparatus to manipulate traffic lights. In subsequent searches on both sides of the border more than 100 terrorists were arrested in France, and 60 in Spain. Later, Inaks Pujana assumed the appointment as ETA-M's Director of Operations.

In Saragossa, 1987 had begun with a car-bomb explosion, which killed two and injured 40, one being a blind lottery ticket-seller; and ended with another alongside a building housing Civil Guard families, which killed two men, two young wives and five young children. Otherwise, terrorist activity in the Spanish Basque region consisted mainly of small explosions. The UATC was jubilant, boasting that during 1987, a year in which 53 terrorist-related deaths had occurred, it had broken up twelve terrorist commando teams.

French Interest Wanes The French authorities began to lose their enthusiasm for co-operation with Spain, and at the October 1987 Summit Meeting, President Mitterrand rejected the Spanish request for joint operations against ETA terrorists, saying 'The Basque Problem is a Spanish Problem.' Mitterrand had plenty of his own terrorist problems by this time and did not want any more; moreover he had elections to face, when a destabilized Basque population would not be to his advantage. He pointed out that he had already returned more than 200 ETA suspects to Spain, and deported others to third countries.

However, Mitterrand continued his efforts to clean up his own Iparretarrak problem, and in February 1988, after a massive security sweep ending in a gun-battle in the mountain village of St-Etienne-de-Baïgorry, Philippe Bidart, founder and leader of the Iparretarrak Basque terrorist organization in France, was arrested, together with two other senior members. Bidart was wanted for killing four policemen. The French boasted that the Iparretarrak was now completely dismantled, and urged the only remaining activist still at large, Lucienne Fourcade, to give herself up. The previous month, French police had arrested Inaki Pujana in Angoulême, near Bordeaux; this may have led them to Bidart.

Continuing the Struggle?

The Removal of Txomin Txomin was arrested by the French police in April 1986, and after being held in custody for a while, was deported to Gabon, from where, with a group of supporters, he eventually made his way to Algeria, the Government allowing him to establish an HQ there. Txomin had lost contact with a majority of his ETA-M members, and his authority over them was being eroded by the fact of his replacement living in French territory; but he did retain some influence and resumed his negotiations with the Spanish Government.

Txomin was killed in a road accident in Algeria in February 1987, and two senior ETA-M leaders riding in the vehicle with him were injured. The Spanish Government allowed his body to be brought back to his home-town of Mondragon, but only on condition that his two injured lieutenants were extradited from Algeria. Txomin, who had been one of the first ETA terrorists to be expelled from France without judicial review, had lost most of his real authority, although he retained considerable influence as a Father Figure of ETA. Had he lived on to regain authority, he would have been a steadying and moderating influence on the now embittered remnants of his old organization.

With Txomin out of circulation, the struggle for the leadership of the ETA-M was won by 'Artapalo', Francisco Mugaica Garmendia, a veteran hardliner, who was against all negotiation with the Spanish Government. He brushed aside all Txomin's directives and policies, complaining that he had never really had a firm grip on the organization. Artapalo believed in the armed struggle, and argued that civilian targets were more profitable than military officers.

Under Artapalo's leadership, ETA-M terrorist activity was stepped up in 1986. In October, General Rafael Garrido Gil, Military Governor of Guipuzcoa Province, was killed in San Sebastian with his wife and son, when an armoured vehicle in which they were riding was halted at a traffic light. Terrorists quickly placed a bomb on the roof of the car, the only part of it not protected by armour-plating.

Yoyes the Traitor Artapalo also cracked down hard on those former ETA members who had accepted the Government's 'Social Integration'; considering them to be traitors, he sought retribution wherever he could. He ordered the 'execution' of Yoyes, and his assassins went to Ordozoa; in September 1986 they shot her while she was playing with her young son in the town square. Txomin had been unable to protect her; Artapalo was creating his own atmosphere. No witnesses could be produced, and few attended her funeral. ('Kubati', José Lopez Ruiz, who fired the bullet that killed Yoyes, was arrested in November 1987.)

That was not the end of Yoyes, who had kept a voluminous diary throughout; she had accumulated a huge dossier of information about ETA, its personnel and operations, which had all been left with her lawyer. Extracts of this work have already been published, to the acute embarrassment of many ETA members and the Government. She gave her reason for quitting her terrorist organization as being in 'the best interests of the Basque Homeland'.

ETA-M Cease-Fire Suddenly, in January 1988, through the columns of *Ergin*, the ETA-M leadership offered an unconditional '60-day Cease-Fire', the first ever from this faction. The attitude of the Spanish Government, riding high at this moment, feeling that ETA was in its death-throes anyway, was cold and suspicious; a feeling justified the following day when an already primed car-bomb was discovered by the police in Bilbao, and two more were found in San Sebastian. In fact, ETA-M seemed set to continue terrorism, within its restricted means; and in March, killed a retired Air Force General, Luis Perez Caballero, as he was leaving church in Vitoria; the same day the Spanish Commando caused an explosion near a Madrid football stadium, that injured two women; and in May, a 'repentant', Sebastian Aispiri, was killed outside his restaurant in San Sebastian.

In February 1988 the Spanish Commando kidnapped a wealthy industrialist, Emiliano Revilla, the purpose being the dual one of blackmailing the Spanish Government into breaking contact with the ETA-M 'HQ' in Algeria, which it had been trying to play off against the Artapalo faction; and to obtain a record ransom. The following day the Spanish Government did break off all contacts with the Algerian faction. The ransom demanded was one billion Spanish pesetas and despite denials, it was rumoured this was being paid quietly and secretly by the family.

In April 1988, José Felix Perez Alonso, believed to be the ETA-M Finance Director, was arrested by the French police at Bayonne, having been under surveillance for some time. He was carrying more than one billion pesetas; controversy arose as to whether this huge sum of money was the Revilla ransom, or the secret ETA-M funds, which Perez Alonso was simply taking to a new hide-out.

Terrorists without a Role? Deprived largely of its French sanctuary, after a 20-year armed struggle, the ETA organization is now factionalized, and partly moribund. The Spanish UATC boasts that only about 30 active terrorists remain at large in Spain and France, while the 'HQ' faction in Algeria has less than 40 supporters; 500 ETA members are still in prison, and the 'Social Integration' scheme is gathering momentum. But there must be reservations in accepting these claims, not least being the new French attitude of non-cooperation in anti-terrorist operations. Not only does a hard core of ETA-M activists exist, but it is supported by a hard core of sympathizers, as exampled in June 1988, when an ETA activist died in prison, and sympathizers set fire to buses and trains in Basque cities.

The Government refuses to accept a 'negotiating process' or the demand to cease Spanish-French anti-terrorist co-operation. It believes that the ETA-M leadership is divided between those, like Artapalo, who want to continue the armed struggle for independence, and those who want to negotiate for the release of the imprisoned, and are content to accept autonomy; at least for the present. The Government refuses to allow terrorists who have committed 'blood crimes' – about one-quarter of those detained – to be admitted into the Social Integration scheme.

The six Basque political parties represented in the Regional Assembly have at last, reluctantly on the part of some, all condemned terrorism. The Civil Guard and National Police are being demilitarized, and given modern training and equipment; and the UATC has acquired considerable counter-terrorist expertise. Basque terrorism is being thrown back to the Basque people themselves, increasingly for the Ertzantza to cope with. It remains to be seen whether the Basques in Spain will remain content with their autonomy, and build on it; or whether the age-old ideal of national independence will still smoulder, perhaps erupting volcano-like again one day. Nationalism and Independence are powerful motivating factors for a terrorist organization.

July 1983, and the body of Dursun Aksoy, an attaché at the Turkish Embassy in Brussels, lies in his car after he was shot and killed by a gunman near his home. The Armenian Secret Army for the Liberation of Armenia claimed responsibility: it was a typical ASALA target and their standard method of operation. (Popperfoto)

6. The Armenian Problem

'*There will be no Armenian Question for 50 years.*' – Talaat Pasha: 1916

THE year 1980 was an active one for Armenian terrorist groups which carried out some 38 attacks on Turkish and Western targets; an increase of nine over the previous year. These included the assassinations of Turkish diplomats in Athens and Sydney; attempted assassinations in Berne, Copenhagen and Rome; and bombing attacks against Turkish, Swiss and Soviet property in London, Los Angeles, New York, Paris, Rome and Brussels. By the end of December, eleven Turkish diplomats had been killed, and several wounded, by terrorists, and a posting abroad for a Turkish diplomat had become a 'high risk' posting.

The first Armenian terrorist exploit in recent years happened on 27 January 1973, in California when a 76-year-old Armenian, Kourken Yanikian, walked into a Santa Barbara hotel, and shot dead both the Turkish Consul-General and the Turkish Consul. This created no special interest at a time when many tiny terrorist groups, with obscure designations and often even more obscure aims, were scrambling to join in the huge swell of international terrorism and anxious to attract attention. In that decade, Turkey had its full share of terrorist groups.

There were no recorded exploits by Armenian terrorists during the following year; but in 1975, there were six, two of which attracted international attention. The first, in January, was an explosion at the HQ of the World Council of Churches in Beirut, responsibility being claimed by the 'Armenian Secret Army for the Liberation of Armenia' (ASALA); and the other, in October, was the assassination of the Turkish Ambassador in Vienna, responsibility being claimed by the 'Justice Commandos of the Armenian Genocide' (JCAG).

In each case the terrorists' demand had been for the restoration of their former 'Homeland' in eastern Turkey. This revival of what had come to be regarded as a long-forgotten lost cause produced vague astonishment everywhere. Suddenly, a 'third generation' was re-activating old demands with a vengeance. Turkey, a member of the United Nations and the NATO alliance, refused either to recognize or negotiate with Armenian terrorists.

There was only one recorded incident in 1976, the killing of a Turkish diplomat in Beirut; but there were eight in 1977, nine in 1978, and a jump to 29 in 1979. In 1981, there were 47 exploits for which Armenian terrorists claimed responsibility, in pursuance of seemingly unattainable demands.

The Armenians: An Ancient People

Armenians have an ancient culture, language and history that goes back to the 6th century, BC, inhabiting a mountainous area that now lies within the confines of eastern Turkey and the Soviet Socialist Republics of Armenia and Azerbaijan. The

Armenians were the first nation to adopt Christianity, in AD 301, as their State Religion. In the Middle Ages the boundaries of the 'Kingdom of Armenia', which enjoyed various degrees of sovereignty and survived onslaughts from Mongols, Persians and Kurds; expanding or contracting depending upon the fortunes of war. The last Armenian State to be formed (with one later brief exception) in AD 1080, was not in Armenia proper, but on the Cilician Plain, near Adana, on the Turkish Mediterranean coast. In 1375 Armenia came under the authority of the expanding Ottoman Empire, Armenians becoming just another Christian minority in a Muslim Empire, like the Assyrians, Chaldeans or Maronites. In about 1826, the eastern part of Armenia, with Armenian approval, came under Russian rule.

During the middle and late 19th century whiffs of nationalism swept through Turkey affecting minorities; a few Armenian activists secretly began forming political groups and voicing demands for an independent Armenia. One such organization was the 'Dashnag-Sution' (Armenian Revolutionary Federation), founded in Tiflis, in adjacent Georgia (then Tzarist territory) in 1890.

The Ottoman Government was ruthless in suppressing and punishing separatist sedition, and several thousand Armenians were killed for this reason in 1884–5. At about this time Armenian activists began to use strong-arm tactics to wrest power from their pro-Ottoman leaders; some of them had served, or were serving, the Ottoman Empire loyally and well until then. It was almost as if they were provoking a direct confrontation under the belief that the great Christian Powers, especially Russia, would come to their aid as a persecuted minority and that the 'Sick Man of Europe' would have to give way.

Next, Armenian activists resumed traditional feuding with their old enemies, the Muslim Kurds, whose communities were interspersed with those of other minorities in eastern Turkey. When the 'Young Turks' came to power in 1909, they laid a heavy hand on suspected Armenian separatists, and are reputed to have killed 30,000 in Adana city, and surrounding villages, and deported others from the Cilician Plain into the eastern interior.

The Massacre In October 1914, Turkey joined Germany and the Austro-Hungarian Empire, to declare war on Britain, France and Russia. The Turkish Minister of the Interior, Talaat Pasha, one of the Triumvirate of Young Turks who ruled the Empire, offered the Armenians autonomy if they would openly side with Turkey, and foment dissent in the Russian part of Armenia; but the pro-Russian political leaders of Armenia refused; they did not trust the Young Turks, and in any case by this time they were demanding full Independence.

Infuriated, Talaat Pasha ordered the 'elimination of the Armenian element which has been trying for centuries to undermine the foundations of our State'. In early 1915, he ordered mass deportation of Armenians from Turkish Armenia to Syria and Mesopotamia, then part of the Ottoman Empire; a process which began in April. Estimates vary widely, but it is probable that there were about 1,800,000 Armenians living in Turkey. A massacre began in the city of Van, the traditional Armenian capital (of which an old Armenian proverb says 'Van in this life and Paradise in the next'), followed by an exodus 'Death March'. Old Van and its ancient churches were destroyed, and the area was left bare and desolate. Again figures are either inflated by emotion or deflated by vested interests; but it is usually estimated that about one-third of the Armenians in this pogrom were killed, another third were deported, and perhaps one-third remained in other parts of

Turkey. The Kurdish tribes took a full part in this murder and harassment, ensuring the emnity of Armenians for many years to come.

Talaat Pasha was later reported to have declared, 'There will be no Armenian Question for 50 years.' He was prophetic.

Dashnag Republic of Armenia: 1918–20 Allied Powers had taken an interest in the misfortunes of the Christian Armenians in Turkey, and indeed other minorities in the Middle East, such as the Kurds, giving them hopes of ultimate independence. On 20 May 1918, the 'Republic of Armenia' was declared in chaotic eastern Turkey. It managed to survive briefly amid appalling famine and privation. US President Wilson's delineation of the 'Armeno-Turkish' Frontier in November 1920, envisaged the new Republic encompassing an area of about 40,000 square miles.

Meanwhile, in Russia there had been Revolution. The Bolsheviks moved into the Caucasus area, and in late 1920 formed what became the Soviet Socialist Republic (SSR) of Armenia. Under the Treaty of Kara in October 1920, between the future Soviet Union and Turkey, the Russians ceded the 'Kara and Ardhan' area to Turkey. This reduced the extent of the Republic of Armenia, and made it more vulnerable in the face of imminent Turkish re-occupation, forcing it to dissolve itself on 2 November 1920. All Armenian territory east of the new Turkish border fell into the Armenian SSR, which became the fifteenth, and smallest of the Republics in the Soviet Union. A change of Allied attitudes and policies resulted in the abandonment of many promises, and the Treaty of Lausanne in 1923 confirmed Turkish sovereignty over the disputed 23,000 square miles of Armenia, thus internationally obliterating the so-called 'Dashnag Republic'. Kemal Atatürk, leading a revival of his defeated country, declared Turkey to be a Republic in October 1923; forcibly re-occupied his Armenian territory; stamped heavily on all traces of separatism; and moved Muslim Kurdish tribes into former Armenian-inhabited areas.

There was just one sting in the Armenian tail, when Dashnag formed a terrorist network, known as 'Nemesis'. In March 1921, it killed Talaat Pasha, then living in Berlin under the alias 'Ali Sayi Bey'; then the former Turkish Foreign Minister, Said Salim, in Rome, the same year; and later in 1923, two other former senior Ottoman officials who had been involved in the Armenian massacres and death march. Nemesis then faded into obscurity. The archetypal Armenian terrorist, upon whom others tried to model themselves, in theory at least, was Soghoman Tehlirian, who had calmly walked up to Talaat Pasha in a Berlin street, drawn a pistol, shot and killed him, put his pistol down, and then waited to be arrested. Tehlirian's case dragged on through the German Courts for years, and he was eventually released, having achieved the status of a hero of Armenian Justice.

Diaspora Meanwhile, the Armenian diaspora sought new homes in foreign countries, forming ethnic communities in Middle Eastern States and western countries, perpetrating their culture, religion, history and sorrows. Armenian political groups, including the Dashnag which had survived, tried to interest governments in their tragedy, and to present their case to the League of Nations, but without success. The exiles, and their first and second generations seemed resigned to their fate, being primarily concerned with building new homes and new lives in new surroundings. The lack of Armenian political success between the two world wars was typified by Hitler's comment, made at a press interview, at Obersalzberg, on 22 August 1939: 'Who, after all, speaks today of the annihilation of the Armenians?'

Well over 150,000 Armenians had settled in Lebanon, then a multi-racial, multi-religious haven for dispossessed minorities. Most resided in East Beirut, the Christian part of the capital, which quickly developed into an Armenian cultural centre of the Diaspora. The tranquility of Lebanon was violently disrupted in 1970–1, when elements of the Palestine Liberation Organization (PLO) were ejected from Jordan, and moved into West Beirut, the Muslim part of the capital, and southern Lebanon, from where they carried out guerrilla raids into Israel. The PLO's flair for attracting world attention by spectacular aircraft hijacking and other notorious acts, began to impress, and then enflame, restless individuals of the third generation of Armenian youth, giving them the thirst for justice and revenge.

The total Armenian population (according to the London-based Minority Rights Group, Report No. 32, 1982) was estimated to be about 6.5 millions, of which about 2.6 millions were in the Armenian and Azerbaijani SSRs. The remainder were scattered across the world, some 500,000 residing in Middle East States; 400,000 in the USA; 200,000 in France; 30,000 in Canada; 25,000 in Bulgaria: 13,000 in Australia; 6,000 in Britain; and so on, with less than 160,000 remaining in Turkey.

Armenian political parties, of which Dashnag was still the most prominent, were impressed by recompense made to the Jews by the West Germans after the war, and formulated their new demands more precisely. Basically these were three. The first was to reclaim their lost 'Homeland' in eastern Turkey, as specified by the Treaty of Sèvres. The second was to seek reparations from Turkey, similar to those made by a defeated Germany to Israel. The third was to seek a Turkish national admission of collective guilt for the crime of 'Genocide against the Armenian people', as Israelis, with American help, had persuaded the Western Allies to force the West German nation to do. In 1975, a coalition of Armenian political parties launched a joint appeal to the United Nations to condemn Turkey, and force the Turkish Government to comply with the three main Armenian demands. The continual Turkish reply to this pressure was the standard, 'We do not have an Armenian Problem, and are not going to create one by talking about it.' The failure of the Turks even to comment, or enter into a dialogue, allowed Armenian publicity to go uncontradicted, which was to the Turkish disadvantage in this propaganda struggle.

A Violent New Generation

Civil war came to Lebanon in April 1975, basically between Maronite Christian and Muslim militias, which devolved into a general fracas, as Palestinian and other militias became involved. For their own protection, like other communities and sects, the Armenians formed three separate militias, the largest being that of Dashnag.

Influenced by the shock-waves reverberating across the world from Palestinian terrorist exploits, two Armenian terrorist groups surfaced independently of each other, to enforce the 'Three Demands' by violence. One group was the 'Justice Commando of the Armenian Genocide' (JCAG), whose leaders adhered to a philosophy of scientific socialism, and was assumed to be the military arm of the Dashnag, although Dashnag traditional philosophy was broadly a right-wing nationalist one. Even so, the JCAG was mainly funded by individual rich Armenians.

After killing the Turkish Ambassador in Vienna in October 1975, and then the Turkish Ambassador in Paris two days later, JCAG issued a communiqué to 'All

Peoples and Governments', stating that it would only lay down its arms when Turkey complied with the Three Demands. A later JCAG communiqué in October 1980 claimed that the object of its terrorist exploits was not revenge, but to extract an admission of guilt from the Turkish Government. Its subsequent communiqués insisted its targets were Turks and Turkish institutions only, and were reprisal measures for injustice against Armenians.

The other terrorist organization was the 'Armenian Secret Army for the Liberation of Armenia' (ASALA), its founder-member being Hagop Hagopian, a young revolutionary with immense dedication and energy, whose long-term aims reached beyond the Armenian Problem, which he considered to be but a step on the path to International Revolution. A Marxist-Leninist, he sought contacts with extreme left-wing revolutionary groups, such as the Turkish Communist Party (TCP) and the Kurdish Workers' Party (KWP); and made fruitful contact with the Popular Front for the Liberation of Palestine (PFLP), and the Democratic Popular Front for the Liberation of Palestine (DPFLP), both of which were extremely left wing, and both of which were then operating out of West Beirut.

ASALA and these two PLO groups collaborated with one another, the Palestinians giving ASALA arms, training and some funding. During the civil war in Lebanon, when the Maronite Falange Militia used the Armenian sector in East Beirut to bombard Palestinians in West Beirut, Hagopian took his ASALA group across what became known as the 'Green Line', the thoroughfare dividing Christian East and Muslim West Beirut, and fought with the Palestinians for the remainder of that war, in the process becoming largely divorced from the East Beirut Armenian community.

ASALA subscribed to the Three Demands, but differed from the JCAG in that it did not confine itself to Turkish targets. ASALA placed heavy emphasis on left-wing revolutionary indoctrination in order to be ready for world revolution one day. ASALA stated in its revolutionary communiqués: 'We will kill and destroy because that is the only language understood by Imperialists.' ASALA later went even further; it was revealed in documents seized by French police, and produced at the trial of top ASALA leader, Monte Melkonian, in December 1986, that in 1981 ASALA members had carried out attacks on targets in Europe which included the Armenian Cultural Centre, and an Armenian church, both in Paris, responsibility for which had been claimed by the fictitious 'Turkish Islamic Army'. the object being to arouse anti-Turkish feelings within the Armenian French community.

Although neither had any direct contact with the other, there was a certain amount of rivalry between the ASALA and the JCAG. For example, when the media wrongly attributed responsibility for terrorist explosions against Swiss targets in Madrid during December 1980 to the JCAG, a JCAG spokesman telephoned an indignant denial, insisting that his organization hit only Turkish targets. Again in Sydney, the same month, a woman telephoned a local newspaper to emphasize that the killing of a Turkish Consul and his bodyguard, was a JCAG responsibility, and had nothing at all to do with ASALA.

On the other hand, in Rome in April 1980, when the JCAG had attempted to assassinate the Turkish Ambassador to the Vatican, claiming responsibility under the code-name of the 'Avengers of the Armenian Genocide', a hooded Hagopian complained in an interview given to a magazine, that 'Dashnag (meaning the JCAG) is trying to imitate us in order to regain lost ground'.

During this period both the ASALA and the JCAG were still pro-Soviet in their general attitude, as were most Armenian political parties, considering the Armenian SSR to be 'Free Armenia', despite its political shortcomings, and their best hope for cultural survival. In the 1920s, Stalin had brought in many dispersed Armenians, even sending ships to Beirut to collect any exiles wanting to settle in the Armenian SSR. In the Soviet Republic Armenians were allowed to use their own language and have it taught in schools, and practise their own religion, but within strict limits. In 1965, the 50th Anniversary of the Genocide, Armenian demonstrators obtained Soviet permission to erect a Monument to the Armenian Genocide in Yerevan, the capital.

On the other hand, the Kremlin leadership stamped heavily on any Armenian political agitation, and certainly did not want the Armenian SSR to become a sanctuary for Armenian terrorists, or a jumping-off place for their activities in adjacent Turkey. Within Turkey, the military *coup* of 1980 led to strict suppression of subversive groups, and all Armenian activists were either imprisoned or hastily fled the country. None were allowed in to the Armenian SSR. The rigid Soviet attitude gradually dampened the original enthusiasm and support from Armenian exiles which had existed. The fact that the Armenian SSR existed at all, tended to mitigate against public support for a Homeland in Turkey, but conversely, tended to encourage support from Armenian exiles for the Three Demands.

Although only two main Armenian terrorist organizations were active, different operational code-names were used by them for some time, to confuse security forces as to the exact numbers of groups involved in terrorism, and their identities. One example was the ASALA 'October 3 Organization', so-called because on 3 October 1980, an explosive device being assembled in a hotel bedroom in a Geneva hotel, blew up causing Arn Yenikomejian to lose his sight and a hand; but his female companion, Suzy Mahseredjian, a 27-year-old Californian law student, escaped injury. Both were brought to trial, and while in custody ASALA organized a series of terrorist explosions, about eighteen in all, in Paris, Madrid and Milan, against Swiss targets, mainly office buildings, to obtain their release. Responsibility was claimed by the 'October 3 Organization'. Both terrorists were convicted of illegal possession of arms and explosives and the woman additionally of obtaining money from Armenians by extortion.

Another was the 'June 9 Organization', so-called after that day in 1981, when Mardiros Jamgodidjian, an ASALA terrorist, was arrested in the act of killing a Turkish diplomat, Mehmet Yergov, outside the Turkish Consulate in Geneva. Later, Jamgodidjian alleged that he thought his victim was a secret police agent. During his period in custody, before conviction, the 'June 9 Organization' carried out fifteen attacks against Swiss targets world-wide. Jamgodidjian's father told the Court, 'We have brought up Mardiros to become a soldier of our nation'; while Armenians in Court chanted 'Asal' (ASALA). When the sentence of fifteen years' imprisonment was pronounced, an Armenian stood up and shouted 'You will have fifteen years of misfortune in Switzerland.' The June 9 Organization then changed its name to the 'Swiss-Armenian Group-15'; which carried out 15 more attacks against Swiss targets.

Another frequently used code-name was the 'Orly Organization', for a team formed after the arrest of four Armenian terrorists who had taken over the Turkish Embassy in Paris during September 1981, to pressure the French authorities into releasing them. Its exploits included an explosion in an automatic luggage locker in

Paris in January 1982, causing considerable damge, but no casualties; exploding a device outside a crowded café in Paris in July, injuring fifteen people; and on the same day, causing an explosion in the just vacated apartment of ex-Marxist revolutionary, Regis Debray, who had been appointed President Mitterand's Special Adviser on Counter-Terrorism; a variation was a 'claimed' explosion on the Paris-Toulouse express train in March 1982 which killed five people (also claimed by other organizations).

Operations and Tactics For the first five years of the decade Armenian terrorist exploits were simple, being mainly explosions or sabotage that did not require much careful planning, or complicated organizational back-up; while 'hard targets', that is protected ones, seemed to be avoided. Devices, mostly using Czech-manufactured plastic Semtex-H, were left in buildings, or outside them, timed to explode at an hour when no lives were endangered, but damage to property would result. These included, a suitcase-bomb left in an empty room at the Law Courts in Geneva in November 1980, by the October 3 Organization, which caused extensive damage, but no injuries to persons; an incident in London in December 1980, when two devices, each with about one pound of explosives packed into a sugar packet, were placed outside the Office of the French Railways and the French Tourist Office. Both had faulty mechanisms, and as the October 3 Organization had made a premature claim of success by telephone to the media, the police were able to defuze them in time.

Shootings were also simple, the target persons usually being in vehicles stationary at traffic lights, slowing down to turn at an inter-section; or parked; or when an individual was on foot. Assassination teams consisted of from two to four terrorists, with either a get-away vehicle nearby, or in, or adjacent to, a crowded thoroughfare. For example, two JCAG terrorists in Rome in April 1980 stopped the car of the Turkish Ambassador to the Vatican travelling along a busy street, fired into the vehicle, wounding him, and then turning quickly to disappear into the crowd.

In Paris a year later two Armenian gunmen approached a Turkish diplomat, Resat Morali, who had just stepped into his car, shot, and killed him; and then shot his companion, Arn Tecelli, a Muslim cleric, through the car-window, and wounded; him while a third Turkish diplomat escaped by taking refuge in a nearby café. The two attackers quickly escaped on foot into an adjacent crowded boulevard. Responsibility was claimed by the 'Armenian Revolutionary Army' (ARA), a code-name that came to be used frequently by ASALA, which issued a communiqué in Beirut, saying 'Our struggle is against the Fascist Regime, and will continue until the liberation of Armenian territory is completed.' Morali was the third such Turkish diplomat to be killed in Paris. Many other Turkish diplomats have been killed or injured in similar terrorist incidents around the world since then.

There were two exceptions in the early, 'simple' stage of Armenian terrorism when hard targets were hit, and both were failures. The first was in Rotterdam in July 1982, being an attempt to kill the Turkish Consul, who was travelling in an armour-plated car, with a two-car police escort. Two gunmen, one on each side of the street, fired several shots, but their 9mm bullets did not pentrate the armour. One terrorist, Benjamin Evingulu, was shot by the police and wounded, but the other escaped. Their failure had been due to lack of research and careful planning.

The other incident was when four ASALA terrorists of the 'Yaya Kashakan Suicide Commando' seized the Turkish Consulate in Paris in September 1981

(Operation 'Van'), killing a security guard, and taking 51 people hostage. The acting Consul was wounded, as was one terrorist, who immediately surrendered to the police. A 15-hour police siege was successfully terminated with the surrender of the three remaining terrorists, who demanded political asylum. Police patience and persistence had been the key to this security forces success. The terrorists had demanded the release of certain political prisoners held in Turkey, but the Turkish Government stated it held no Armenian political prisoners.

The International Situation   Gaston Defferre, French Minister of the Interior, said in April 1982 that France would give moral support to Armenian national groups, and permission was given for a monument to the Armenian Genocide to be erected near Paris, which upset the Turkish Government, already critical of French leniency towards Armenian terrorists. Max Kilindjian, an ASALA terrorist, had been acquitted of killing a Turkish Ambassador in January 1982 by a French Court. On arrival in Beirut, Kilindjian was presented triumphantly at an ASALA press conference. Also, the four Armenians who had forced their way into the Turkish Consulate, were granted political asylum. Turkish protests were low key, because the Turks did not want a major confrontation with France, as they would have lost out on the Human Rights issues, and perhaps even forfeited their seat in the Council of Europe. When the French released Kilindjian, ASALA declared a truce with the French Government, but this ended abruptly in July, just after the arrest of Vicken Charkutian, another ASALA member, in France, and his subsequent extradition to Los Angeles, to answer terrorist charges there. An ASALA communiqué of July 1982, issued in Beirut, declared a resumption of 'military acts against the interests of France, Switzerland, Canada, the United States, Belgium, Holland and Sweden'.

One of the more notorious ASALA exploits occurred at Orly Airport, Paris, on 23 July 1983, when a suitcase-bomb left on a luggage trolley near the check-in desks in the crowded departure lounge exploded, killing eight people and injuring another 55. The device had contained about one pound of explosives attached to a canister of domestic heating gas, which accounted for a number of serious burns. The police drag-net brought in more than 50 Armenians, of whom four were charged with this crime and another eleven were deported. The leader of this terrorist team, code-named the 'Orly Organization', Varadjian Garbidian, reputed to be the Head of ASALA in France, was one of those charged, the other three being Ionnes Semerci, Nayir Somer, and Aram Basmadjian. This was considered to be a major success for the French security forces, although the American CIA also claimed to have infiltrated the Orly Organization. Armenian groups world-wide condemned this indiscriminate carnage of civilians, as did the second Armenian World Congress, then in session at Geneva.

Internal Rivalries: Moderates versus Extremists   There had been dissension within ASALA for some time, and the Orly Airport explosion was the catalyst that brought about a split within it. Still led by the fanatical Hagop Hagopian, ASALA had been based in West Beirut, receiving Palestinian and other revolutionary aid, until driven from that city by the Israeli invasion of southern Lebanon in June 1982, and the subsequent prolonged Israeli bombardment of the Muslim part of the city. It was given out that Hagopian had been killed in this bombardment, which later proved not to be so, but at the time, and subsequently, this was generally considered to be a probability. No current authenticated photograph of him seemed to exist, but this was due perhaps to the tight cell secrecy of the leadership echelon of ASALA; Hagop Hagopian had always appeared shrouded in a hood at his several press conferences.

It is probable that Hagopian left West Beirut, after an internal power struggle within ASALA, went to the Beka'a Valley in Lebanon, and adopting the alias of 'Mihran Mihranian' (another was reputed to be 'Vahram Vahramian) he moved to Syria, to a training camp near Homs, then used by several left-wing revolutionary and terrorist groups. After that he seems to have been continually on the move, reputedly visiting Cyprus, Greece and certain Middle Eastern and North African States. Hagopian seemed to be successful in obtaining funds from Colonel Gaddafi of Libya.

Within ASALA moderates had long been at loggerheads wtih the extremists, the latter still having world revolution in their sights. They had been accusing Hagopian of deliberately sending terrorists on suicide-missions to gain favour with Gaddafi and obtain more funds; and also objected to his close relationship with Abu Nidal's radical Fatah-General Council.

Two extremist protagonists were executed by moderates; and in turn two moderates were killed by extremists, thus making the cleavage within ASALA deep and lasting. The moderates formed themselves into the 'ASALA-Revolutionary Movement' (ARM), sometimes written as 'ASALA-RM', which in its first communiqué of September 1983 accuses ASALA leaders of being gangsters and dictators; and of attacking targets with the deliberate intention of causing indiscriminate death and injury. ARM policy was to move slowly back into Turkey, in furtherance of the ultimate aim of a 'Free Armenia'; and to link up again with the discontented Turkish (TCP) and Kurdish (KWP) groups instead of consorting with Palestinian and other international terrorist organizations.

ARM became the military wing of the 'Democratic Front for the Liberation of Armenia' (DFLA), but while ARM had a majority of former ASALA members, ASALA retained the arms, money, organization, international terrorist contacts, and dedicated, ruthless leadership. A smaller, tighter ASALA, still led by the shadowy Hagopian and his hard-line revolutionaries, retained their Syrian and Iraqi links, and accused the ARM of being a 'tool of Turkish Imperialism and the American CIA'. By this time few Armenians seemed to resent the Kurdish role in their Genocide, accepting that the Kurds had been manipulated by the 'Young Turks'.

Three Armenian political parties, each with a terrorist wing, had survived, continuing to operate mainly from East Beirut, with tentacles reaching into the Western world. The main one was still the Dashnag, reputed still to have strong links with the JCAG; the small Huntchak, which was a rather lethargic left-of-centre group; while the more active DFLA, which had originally supported ASALA, and in February 1983 had made that support conditional to its stepping-up terrorist activity inside Turkey in September, began instead to back the ARM; and indeed ARM soon gained considerable popularity within the Armenian diaspora.

Because of changing allegiances, there was feuding between Armenian groups, both political and terrorist, and one minor Armenian terrorist organization, the New Armenian Resistance Movement (NARM), led by Aran Turunian, clashed with ASALA. A device was discovered under Turunian's car in Paris in March 1983, and he narrowly escaped with his life when it exploded. There were other attempts on Turunian's life, but all failed.

Taking the Campaign to Turkey The first major terrorist exploit in Turkey since the military *coup* was carried out by ASALA on 7 August 1982 (before that organization was split asunder) by the 'Pierre Gulumian Commando'. Two members, Levan Ekmekciyan and Zouhrab Sarkissian, attacked the Esenboga Airport, near Ankara. (Pierre Gulumian had been killed in Paris in July 1982, when assembling a bomb that blew up prematurely.) The attack began with two grenades being thrown into the departure lounge, followed by bursts of automatic fire. The two terrorists then moved into the restaurant to hold 23 people there hostage, shooting and killing an American woman who attempted to escape.

Police commandos were rushed to Esenboga, from the capital about 20 miles away, and stormed the restaurant. Sarkissian was killed in an explosion, while Ekmekciyan was captured, convicted and executed in January 1983. At first it was thought there were three terrorists, but the third man turned out be a Turkish student, whose contact lens had dropped out when the first grenade exploded, and who had blindly jumped from the restaurant window. The terrorists' demands, mainly for the release of certain Armenian political prisoners from Turkish gaols, had been passed to the media, but ignored by the security forces, which had been trained to attack rather than negotiate in such situations, regardless of danger to civilians.

The next major ASALA attack in Turkey took place on 16 June 1983, in Istanbul, when a single gunman of the 'Leven Ekmekciyan Suicide Commando', threw a grenade into a crowded street, adjacent to the Lapali Carsi Bazaar, fired his automatic weapon into the covered market, and then threw another grenade, that killed himself and a 13-year-old girl. Some 27 people were injured in this exploit. Owing to mutilation from the grenade blast, the Turkish security forces were never able to identify the assassin. By this time, ASALA also began wildly to exaggerate its claims, and on this occasion, in a communiqué issued from Athens, it claimed its suicide commando had 'killed 27 people, including seventeen Turkish soldiers'. It also warned foreign tourists that, 'Turkey is now a military target for our suicide commandos'. Incidentally, the martyr Ekmekciyan was later discredited by ASALA, it having been discovered that he 'had confessed all to the Turkish authorities after being arrested'.

Meanwhile, the JCAG was also active in several countries, but still attacked only Turkish targets; they killed diplomats in Lisbon, the USA and Canada during 1982 and a defence attaché in Ottowa. A telephone message to an Ottawa newspaper said, 'This is the work of the Justice Commando of the Armenian Genocide. We will strike again.' The victim's daughter said, 'My father lived in fear of such an attack. I always knew. He told us never to go out alone.' A security guard protected the Defence Attaché's residence, but did not accompany him away from it unless the police had warned there might be trouble.

In Burgas, Bulgaria in September 1982, a JCAG terrorist shot dead a Turkish diplomat, and escaped. In Brussels in July 1983, the JCAG claimed one of its gunmen had killed a Turkish diplomat at the Turkish Embassy: but then so did ASALA: neither was above making false claims.

ASALA continued its suicide-missions, and six members of one of its ARA commandos attacked the Turkish Embassy in Lisbon during July 1983, arriving in a van, hired by two men with Libyan passports. The security guard at the main gate was shot dead, and in an exchange of shots, one terrorist was killed. Unable to force their way into the Embassy, the terrorists broke into adjacent residential quarters, a building that was soon surrounded by Portuguese police commandos. The operation, the first of this nature, lasted 45 minutes. An explosion occurred within the building which caught fire, and all five terrorists perished in the flames. The Portuguese authorities had made no attempt to negotiate with them, and the security forces team was about to launch an attack. Also killed was a Turkish diplomat and a diplomat's wife, while another diplomat and a security guard were wounded.

A telephone call to a local media agency, directed attention to a note left on a park bench opposite the Embassy. The police found some children playing with the note, which was written in English; and read. 'We know what we are doing. The Freedom Lobby of Armenian Youth has resolved never to rest. We have lost everything. We have decided to blow up the building and remain under the collapse. This is not suicide, nor an expression of insanity, but rather our sacrifice to Freedom.' An ASALA statement, telephoned to a French journal, said that, 'Two new members have arrived in Lisbon to seek revenge. The Turkish Embassy should prepare for a major attack.'

In Vienna in November 1984, a Turkisk diplomat was shot and killed while driving his car in heavy traffic, his vehicle crashing into another one. The attacker threw a black towel, with the letters 'A.R.A.' prominently marked on it, into the car, before quickly disappearing into an adjacent underground station.

Spectacular ASALA exploits became less frequent, and one of the final ones occurred in Ottawa in March 1985, when three terrorists: Kerverk Marachelian, Rafi Titijian, and Channes Noubarian stormed the Turkish Embassy. They killed a security guard, and held twelve people hostage for four hours before surrendering. The Turkish Ambassador was injured in escaping through a window. Responsibility was claimed by ASALA, and the three terrorists were later convicted and imprisoned in June 1986.

Probably the last significant ASALA act took place in Melbourne in Australia in November 1985, when a car-bomb exploded outside the Turkish Consulate, killing one person, and damaging the building. Responsibility was claimed by the as yet unknown 'Greek-Bulgarian-Armenian Front', but it had all the hall-marks of ASALA; although the JCAG was also suspected.

Extending the Theatre of Operations   Except for a few small explosions, Britain had been relatively free from Armenian terrorism until July 1983, when good co-operation between west European security forces prevented what might have been a main ASALA terrorist *coup*. Only a few days after the Orly Airport explosion, Zavan Bedros, a 32-year-old Syrian-born Armenian, a cousin of the executed Ekmekciyan, who later claimed to be Head of ASALA in Britain and France, posing as a businessman visiting Britain to buy Land Rover spares, immediately came under British police surveillance. Bedros's task was to lead a suicide-commando to seize the Turkish Embassy in London, kill a senior diplomat, take hostages, and demand the release of Armenian political prisoners in Turkey.

Bedros was arrested outside his hotel in London on 9 September, with a companion, Grish Gregorian, four days before he was due to swing into action. Russian pistols, ammunition and grenades were found in his hotel room. He told the police he was the leader of a five-man ASALA Commando (although he later denied this in Court) saying, 'I remember my old grandmother telling me tales of the 1915 Massacre, and asking me when I was going to take up arms to avenge it.' At his trial he said bitterly, 'Whenever I leave prison I want to hit them, everyone; the Turks, the British Government and all foreigners, because they are all traitors.' He later added, 'Death or prison are better for me than failure to do my job.' This outburst was indicative of the inherent fury ot the third-generation Armenian avengers. Bedros was convicted, but his companion was acquitted.

In the early 1980s, ASALA began operating in troubled Iran, its initial exploits consisting of small explosions by the Orly Organization commando. On one occasion it had attempted to kidnap an Italian diplomat, mistaking him for a Turk. The tempo was stepped-up in 1983 when, on 23 July, the Air France Office in Tehran was bombed; and again on the 24th, on 7 August, and on 10 August. In September, an ASALA bomb explosion in a Turkish Embassy car, injured two Turkish employees. An ASALA terrorist, Isil Unel, was killed by the premature explosion of his own bomb, when attaching it to a Turkish diplomat's car in March 1984.

The ASALA Orly Organization commando launched an attack on the Turkish Embassy in Tehran in March 1984, during which a diplomat and a Deputy Defence Attaché were wounded. An Iranian government statement condemned, 'all who attempt to damage Iranian-Turkish relations.' Ayatollah Khomeini's Revolutionary Guards promptly rounded-up and arrested groups of Armenians living in the capital.

ASALA replied that, 'All Middle East States with security links with Turkey, the United States, or Israel; and Airlines serving Turkey, are revolutionary targets.' This was followed by ASALA gunmen shooting dead a Turkish businessman. This was too much for the Iranian authorities, and resulted in more harassment of Armenians in Tehran, and the crushing of ASALA terrorism in that country.

A Futile Struggle?

Turkey's Reactions In March 1983, the Turkish President, Kenan Evran, had called for renewed international efforts in the fight against international terrorism, and that month he personally visited Beirut, to request Lebanese co-operation, as it was widely alleged that the airport was manipulated by international terrorists; but by this time the central government's control was extremely limited; local armed militias in turn seeming to have a grip on the airport areas. Later, in August 1984, the Turkish President again criticized the Lebanese Government for 'allowing Armenian terrorists to board planes in Beirut while armed like arsenals'.

Turkish relations with France remained uneasy, owing to French recognition of the Armenian Genocide, and President Mitterrand's statement on a visit to Austria in January 1984 that, 'It is not possible to cover up the Armenian Genocide.' Three small explosions occurred in May 1984 at the Monument to the Armenian Genocide near Paris, in which twelve people were injured, and the monument slightly damaged. No one claimed responsibility for this act, but the extreme ASALA group was suspected, as it had done this sort of thing before to arouse anti-Turkish feelings among the Armenian diaspora; but also there were rumours that covert Turkish forces had been at work.

In a somewhat unusual statement, Turgut Ozal, the Turkish Prime Minister said in February 1985 that the Armenian incidents had really been a wartime military operation against Russian-backed insurrections; and that the overall death toll had been less than 300,000. He also said that no specific order had ever been issued to kill Armenians, and that the so-called 'Talaat Pasha's instructions' had been falsified; he claimed that there were fewer than 1.5 million Armenians in Turkey at that time. Ozal also pointed out that thousands of Armenians lived in Turkey still, and had freedom of worship, while their Patriarch consistently condemned Armenian violence. The Armenian Patriarch, Chnourk Kaloustjian, of the Armenian Orthodox Church, whose seat was at Istambul, called for a neutral commission to be appointed to study the facts of the Armenian Genocide.

In September 1984 the US House of Representatives voted to designate 24 April as the National Remembrance Day for Man's Inhumanity to Man, which brought protests from President Reagan, who considered Turkey to be a most valuable NATO ally, and did not want to upset its government; and also from American Jewish organizations, which cynics said wanted all emphasis to be concentrated upon the Jewish Holocaust, and did not want to share any 'Remembrance' spotlight with others.

Armenian political pressure continued to be applied in the United States and at the United Nations, resulting in the UN sub-committee on the Prevention of Discrimination and Protection of Minorities accepting a report in August 1985 which stated that at least one million, possibly well over half the Armenian population, were reliably estimated to have been killed, on Death Marches in Turkey in 1915; but refrained from passing judgement, and so the report was referred to the UN Commission on Human Rights. Turkey made its usual protests, but there was a general reluctance on the part of any Western government to condemn outright and affix the blame on Turkey.

The Quiet Years Little of note happened during 1986 in the field of Armenian terrorism, except the release of the three surviving members responsible for the forcible occupation of the Turkish Embassy in Paris in September 1981. When they arrived safely in Greece, ASALA sent a message to Prime Minister Chirac, thanking his government for 'Understanding the struggle and cause of the Armenian people', and for releasing the three comrades from the unjust sentence imposed on them by the Socialist-Imperialist government of President Mitterrand.

The year 1987 was also a quiet one, although it began violently when a postal package exploded at Brisbane injuring six people; ASALA claimed responsibility. In February the (now) Syrian-backed ASALA sent a communiqué to a media agency in Beirut, threatening new bomb attacks against French interests, unless certain Arabs held in French custody were released, one of whom was Georges Ibrahim Abdullah, leader of FARL, who had links with ASALA. Similar threats had been made during the previous October. Nothing had been heard of JCAG activities for some time. The momentum seemed to have gone out of the Armenian terrorist movements, although political pressure to brand Turkey as being guilty of the Armenian Genocide was intensified. It seemed as though the terrorist whirlwind had blown itself out.

Death of Hagopian Suddenly and unexpectedly, news broke that Hagop Hagopian, famed leader of ASALA, who had become a mysterious, shadowy figure (whom most people accepted had probably died, or been killed, somewhere along the line) had been assassinated in Athens on 28 April 1988. Posing as a Yemeni diplomat, he had been shot by an unknown gunman, who escaped. At once there was widespread scepticism as to whether the victim was really Hagopian, but the Greek Government swept aside such speculations, confirming the dead man was indeed Hagopian, and that ample authentication, for example, from his wife, was available. There seemed to be no doubt. Alive, disappeared or dead, Hagopian had been either the mainspring, or inspiration of ASALA. The violent wave of third-generation Armenian terrorism, which had been fading for some time, may have died with him; being simply a phenomenon that adds another unsuccessful chapter to the history of the Armenian diaspora.

No one claimed responsibility for killing Hagopian, but most blamed an ASALA faction. Others alleged that it was a carefully planned Turkish covert operation, and that Turkish undercover agents had been searching for him for months in order to assassinate him. It is known that the Turkish Government admires the Israeli Mossad (Secret Service) and its operations against Palestinian terrorists; and especially the killing of Abu Jihad at the PLO HQ in Tunis. If there is substance in this allegation, which the Turkish Government firmly denies, perhaps Turkish Security Forces were impressed by the clinical way the British SAS eliminated the PIRA 'Gibraltar Three'.

Possible or Impossible Aims?   Terrorism has clearly failed to achieve the Armenian Three Demands. The emphasis is now on international political pressure to obtain them, but there must be soul-searching as to whether they are possible or impossible, to achieve. It might be possible, although extremely doubtful under current circumstances, to coerce the Turkish Government into admitting national guilt for the Genocide, and even persuade it to pay heavy reparations, although the Turkish economy is relatively weak; but it must surely be impossible to restore the Armenians to their claimed 'Homeland' in eastern Turkey.

Since the early 1920s this Homeland has been occupied by Kurds, now demanding Independence for themselves; they can't both have it. Paradoxically, Armenians and Kurds, who have been collaborating in the terrorist field, are competing with each other for the same ultimate political objective. Pre-1915, Armenians had a majority in only one province, that of Van. Today Van is a Kurdish city (old Van has disappeared) suffused with Kurdish nationalism: Armenians do not live there any more. Were such an arrangement possible, returning Armenians would receive a hostile reception, as many Turks are alive today whose grand-parents had been murdered in the racial struggles of those days; and memories are long in eastern Turkey.

The Nagorno-Karabakh Footnote   Information about recent disturbances in the SSRs of Armenia and Azerbaijan, and their demands that the inter-republic frontier be re-adjusted to encompass the Nagorno-Karabakh enclave in the SSR of Azerbaijan, surrounded by a Muslim population, into the Armenian SSR, comes to us in unusual volume by courtesy of Gorbachev's Glasnost policy of openness. Any concessional alteration to inter-republic frontiers would cause ripples of discontent in the Soviet Muslim Central Asian Republics and open up similar controversial demands. One feels that the Kremlin leadership will simply keep pouring ample cold water on the situation to freeze it as much as possible. The effect of the Soviet Armenian disturbances and demonstrations on the almost dormant Armenian terrorists groups will be negative.

7. Thoughts on Counter-Terrorism

'In some countries bodyguards and armour-protected cars are status symbols.'

IN Western democracies terrorists seem to have so much going for them that some governments tend to despair, and try to ignore or shut out the problem, as they have to labour under so many democratic restraints. This is regrettable and can only work in favour of terrorism; everyone should strive in unison against it to the best of their ability. It is most unlikely that terrorism can ever be completely eradicated from world society because there are so many catalysts; but it can be contained at a low level if certain measures are taken. Broadly, these fall into three categories: passive security; expertise of security forces, and international co-operation; but all three must be motivated and activated, by governmental will, and the determination rigidly to enforce them without fear, political expediency, or other exception.

Security Measures

Passive security measures are the 'home defences' against terrorism, the visible and obvious precautions which through their openness are a deterrent in themselves to all but the most determined terrorist. They can be classed as security of property and security of people. In simple form, the first means the installation on property of defences such as wire-perimeter fences or compound walls; steel-shuttered doors and windows, burglar alarms; carefully sited laser-beam warning devices; flood-lighting at night; uniformed security personnel on duty and patrols with guard dogs; and signs boldly indicating that such measures are in force. Installations and buildings should be made to look like 'hard targets' where terrorists would expect to meet alerted resistance, and once committed to action, would probably find all their escape routes blocked.

Private security has become big business in most Western democracies, as industrial organizations, businesses, banks, factories, offices, private residences, and even individuals, can hire visible protection around the clock if required. Private security firms can give special attention to a particular need, and so can concentrate upon a particular site or individual. Police forces, invariably over-stretched, tend to be reactive, and can give only general protection; they cannot be everywhere at once. Private security does not come cheap, and so is limited by the financial ability to pay for it, although much of the cost can usually be off-set against insurance premiums. Governments themselves are big employers of private security to protect embassies, buildings and installations.

To obtain maximum security against terrorism it is important for vulnerable installations and individuals to adopt a few simple security rules and routines. Organizations that employ large numbers of people in the same building or complex, where it is impossible for everyone to know whom everyone else is, should insist that all wear a visible identity card, with photograph and brief data on it, for all to see. Staff entering and leaving the premises should be logged, and side and rear entrances should be secure, and not left open and unmanned. Cleaning and casual staff should not be overlooked in monitoring routines.

There should be a special entrance for visitors, and a reception area where their identity and purpose can be verified, by a telephone call if necessary. Unless restricted to a certain office or area, they should be given a visitor's identity card, or other means of indicating that they are not regular staff. On construction sites, and oil installations, for example, visitors are given different coloured safety helmets to wear. Although an expensive, and perhaps inconvenient, extra, such means will prevent unauthorized persons wandering in and out without being challenged. Most large department stores have such routines to counter large-scale theft.

Terrorists like to 'case a joint' thoroughly, and before they operate against it, familiarize themselves with its lay-out, where the main offices, entrances and exits, alarm systems and power control points are, and what security rules, routines and spot-checks are in operation. Terrorist groups carefully watch airports for weeks prior to mounting an exploit, to detect counter-terrorist measures. Sometimes decoys are sent through check-points carrying a pistol to test detection devices. Strict security routines deter, while lax ones attract.

Airports Perhaps the best-known security routine is searching passengers and their luggage at airports before boarding an aircraft, to ensure that they do not have any arms or explosives in their possession, knowingly or unknowingly. Hand luggage has either to be opened for inspection or put through an electronic scanner; and other luggage usually has to be identified by the owner on the tarmac apron, before it is loaded on to the plane. The object is to stop any potential skyjackers on the ground before they become airborne. This routine has become an accepted necessity at airports even though it is an infringement of civil liberties. Generally, it has been very, but not completely, successful and incidents of skyjacking have fallen off since their heyday in the 1970s; but they still occur.

Some airports are more thorough in their security routines than others, awareness perhaps being sharpened by vulnerability and previous experiences. Israel, for example, remains most thorough in its air travel routines. As checking tasks are invariably tedious, efficiency tends to fluctuate, dependent upon lax or strict supervision, boredom, carelessness, or a false sense of security brought on by lulls in terrorist activity. There is a limit to the length of time one can efficiently watch a monitor screen before vision blurs and dulls, or the mind wanders.

The deterrent value of security routines at airports is obviously considerable, but unfortunately not easily measurable. Detection successes are seldom widely reported as they do not usually make good media copy; and some airports prefer not to publicize such incidents, as they tend to unsettle passengers; but occasionally they do come to light. A notable example was the Irish girl who was persuaded (unwittingly) by an Arab terrorist to take an explosive device on board an Israeli airliner at London Airport. The device was detected on the ground, and so the lives of the 376 people on that aircraft were saved.

On the other hand, 329 lives were lost when an Air India Boeing 747 crashed into the Atlantic Ocean as the result of a terrorist explosion on board. Someone, or something, had been lax in the routine security system at either the Toronto or Montreal airports, where the explosive device must have been put aboard the aircraft. Some airports are notoriously lax, and the finger continually points to Athens, where it is suspected that terrorists have boarded aircraft on stop-overs, and arms and explosives have been smuggled aboard to be used by skyjackers.

Personal Precautions Many individuals, including Ministers, political leaders, senior military officers, or security personnel engaged in the fight against terrorism, may be marked out for assassination, for intimidation purposes, vengeance or example. Rich industrialists, and senior executives of major or multi-national concerns, able and willing to pay large ransoms, or their families, may be kidnapped for ransom. Some who refuse to pay a ransom, or Revolutionary Taxes, are killed, as has happened in Spain by ETA terrorists. In some countries, soldiers and policemen of any rank are assassinated by terrorists, such as the New People's Army 'Sparrow Squads', in Manila, simply to break down confidence in law and order. Others are kidnapped for their political and sometimes for their financial hostage value, such as Westerners by the Hezbollah groups in Lebanon.

Individuals or families at risk from assassination or kidnapping, can take simple precautions that will reduce their vulnerability considerably. They can attend professional security courses in survival, which lay down simple rules to be followed. The first fact to appreciate is that most people are creatures of habit; some men invariably leave home for their office or place of work every day at the same time by the same route and means, and return in a similar manner; habitually using the same shops, clubs, cafés, restaurants and places of leisure. One Spanish police chief always obtained petrol for his car at the same filling station; another always had his breakfast at the same café at the same time every day: both were unconsciously making their own trap into which one day they walked, to find an assassin waiting for them.

Simple ground rules are: vary times of departure, and vary routes. Avoid habit-forming visits to places and people; itineraries of those at risk should be confidential and known only to a trusted few, and information of appointments, timings or dates, or visits should not be made public in advance. The domestic staff at the home of a French General in Paris, told terrorists, when they telephoned to ask, the precise time he would return, with fatal results. Telephone calls asking a person at risk to meet someone somewhere, or collect his children early from school, should be double-checked, and treated with gave suspicion.

Depending upon the status of the person at high-risk, and resources available to him, if not already afforded normal police protection, he will probably hire private bodyguards, and travel in an armour-protected car. This will make him a hard target, especially as in some countries the bodyguards may be armed, so attackers would meet some resistance. Hired bodyguards are familiar sights in some countries, such as Italy; and are also used to guard residences and to protect families, escorting them when away from home, thus making them even harder targets. In some countries bodyguards and armoured-protected cars are status symbols. Even so, high-risk persons should alter routine timings, vary routes, have in-car radio communication and telephones so that their movements can be monitored, and suspicious details reported; have escort vehicles and use decoy vehicles; and avoid busy narrow streets and rush-hour traffic.

The medium-risk and low-risk person who drives his own car should also take simple precautions, which include varying times, routes and routines. He should always keep his car locked; have alarms affixed that will indicate if it has been tampered with in any way; should automatically examine his vehicle for any suspicious sign, and then look underneath it. Failure to look underneath was a fatal omission of the Lisburn Five. Such routines should become habitual.

When driving, car-doors should be locked from the inside to prevent them being suddenly opened by a terrorist if stopped, who might either shoot, drag the victim from the car, or get into the vehicle to hold the driver hostage. Individual drivers should avoid lonely roads where they could be ambushed, or rush-hour traffic when they can be boxed-in and be vulnerable to a terrorist on foot or on a motorcycle. A favourite terrorist tactic, known as 'Shoot-and-Scoot', is for two terrorists on a motorcycle to draw alongside the victim's car when halted by traffic lights, or in dense traffic, enabling the pillion-rider to use his automatic weapon to kill the driver, before speeding away. Some terrorist groups have electronic means to alter traffic-light sequences for this type of tactic. Motorcycle helmets are an almost perfect disguise. A suggestion sometimes put forward is that it should be forbidden for two people to ride on a motorcycle; this happens in Sri Lanka, which also banned motorcycle helmets after one such incident.

Private security firms run courses for drivers of high-risk persons and for low-risk persons who drive their own cars. These teach them to become aware of certain danger signals; of being followed by another vehicle; of potential ambush sites; and if ambushed, how to reverse at speed; and how to avoid or deal with being boxed-in by hostile vehicles. There should always be plenty of fuel in vehicle tanks, to avoid running low on a lonely road, or having to pull into an unfamiliar filling station; and to enable a long detour to be made if suspicious circumstancs arise.

Private security firms also run courses on Hostage Survival, which give instruction and hints on how to stay alive if kidnapped; how to adjust psycho-logically to conditions; not to antagonize kidnappers, or look them in the eye, or give any provocation; but to enter into restrained dialogue with them if possible, to obtain some sort of rapport to reduce tension. Hostages should note and memorize as many details of the kidnappers, the 'prison' in which they are held, external noises, and conversations between terrorists, to help security forces ultimately to track them down. American source figures indicate that more than 80 per cent of kidnapped people survive.

High-risk individuals and families, sometimes have to live under what are virtually siege conditions. The majority of those whose risk assessment varies from being an opportunity target, to a medium-risk one, have to settle for a sensible balance between tight security and freedom of movement. Over-tight security measures which tend to breed a siege-mentality, especially within security forces, with everyone hiding behind locked doors and forever looking apprehensively over their shoulders, should be avoided as far as possible. The aim should be to continue normal life as usual, but with an added awareness; to be always on the look-out for anything suspicious or out of the ordinary, and to report it instantly, or to know how to react to it. As soon as a siege-mentality begins to develop, the initiative moves over to the terrorists.

Security Forces

The best counter to terrorism is to apprehend terrorists and bring them before the Courts, which hopefully should award exemplary sentences. To accomplish this terrorists must first be detected and arrested, and evidence accumulated to ensure conviction, which is the task of security forces, a term that includes police forces of all types; these tend to vary in character, background, training and expertise, from country to country. Their success rate in the battle against terrorism rests to a large extent upon their expertise, which is influenced and motivated by political will, or at least it should be.

Britain and the ROI are almost unique since they have unarmed police, while most other nations arm their police. They concentrate upon what we think of as 'civilian' police tasks; protecting life and property, fighting major crime, dealing with petty crimes, traffic control, and other mundane matters. Some Western countries have both para-military police forces, and armed police forces, while Third World countries usually have a mixture. Some Western countries have more than one force, or agency, for law enforcement, sometimes with blurred divisions between their responsibilities, or even gaps; a state of affairs suitable to a country that fears the development of a police state if too much power is put into too few hands. The problem of international terrorism usually falls on the police, either para-military or civil, who are at times aided by the military.

A few national security forces were quick to recognize the nature of terrorism, and to form specialized sections or teams, to deal with it; others were slow to follow suit, only developing counter-terrorist sections as circumstances forced them to do so. In western Europe in 1980, Belgium, for example, did not have a special counter-terrorist group at all; but soon all Western governments recognized that not only are such groups an absolute necessity, but members of them must have special qualities, aptitudes, skills and training, and sophisticated equipment, essential to enable them to keep one step ahead of international terrorists, whose expertise continually improves with the times.

Intelligence-Gathering A main task of security forces in their active role of combating terrorism, is to obtain, collate and analyse every scrap of information about terrorists, their habits, accomplices, motivations, and indeed anything remotely connected with them that might be the missing piece in the detection jig-saw puzzle. This is stored on central computers which have key-in terminals at airports, frontier posts and police stations, from which instant information can be obtained, or fed in, to up-date computer data. Such computers have now become commonplace and generally acceptable, most governments of liberal democracies having overcome resistance to them from civil rights campaigners, and those who fear the evolution of a police state.

Progress is also being made in instant transmission of finger-prints, photographs and documents, so that neither time, nor terrorists, are lost. Electronic bugs can be affixed to vehicles, weapons, or hidden on people, enabling them to be located and tracked; a most useful device in kidnapping cases. New scientific aids are being harnessed to counter-terrorist techniques, one being 'genetic finger-printing', a means enabling police to identify individuals from genetic make-up of body fluids. Several nations have adopted the West German 'target team' technique, of a small section of men concentrating wholly on one single terrorist to track him down.

A national identity card system for the population is a big asset to security forces in detecting both terrorists, criminals, and drug dealers. Within the EEC, only Britain and the ROI have not adopted this, and because of resistance by civil rights campaigners on this issue, governments are reluctant to introduce it. Most adults in these two countries usually carry some form of identification, such as a driver's licence, a banker's card, or a membership card of some club or organization; so it must be assumed that the introduction of such a system would hardly upset the majority; exceptions being terrorists, and others anxious to evade the attention of the law. Perhaps EEC example, and pressure, may soon rectify this omission.

Training and Assault Techniques Police training nowadays is thorough, highly technical, and includes psychological techniques on how to deal with people, and to question suspects expertly to obtain the maximum information from them. During the mid-1980s, certain Western security forces, including those of France, Italy and Spain, were completely re-organized, re-trained and re-conditioned away from old hampering traditions; a few others were not, and are still dragging their heels in this respect. Greece is a country in which police expertise seems less than satisfactory; for example, practically nothing of any significance is known about the November 17 Organization, and as yet not a single one of its assassins has been brought to justice. Owing to background circumstances and motivation it seems easier for the police to obtain information about local terrorists in some countries than in others. The IRA groups in NI are cursed with informers, while both Italy and Spain seem to be able to obtain an adequate level of intelligence, but in Corsica, the people, whether they agree with the Corsican freedom fighters or not, will not utter a word about them to the French police.

Skyjacks and hostage situations require special techniques; when terrorists make demands, innocent lives are at stake, so the situation must be resolved as soon as possible without bloodshed. Some countries have formed military commandos for this specific purpose, such as Egypt and Pakistan, both of which have an abrupt, hard-line approach, of moving quickly into the assault, the principle of over-powering terrorists obliterating that of the sanctity of human life. The assault by the Egyptian Saiqa on terrorists holding hostages on the Air Egypt airliner at Malta, caused 60 deaths, being the bloodiest result to date; while at Karachi, in September 1986, a military commando enforced a bloody solution on an attempted skyjack situation, that left 22 people dead and another 20 injured.

Most countries now adopt a more humane approach, and the British police lead the field in accepted techniques involving patience, psychology and dialogue in a tussle of strength, stamina and nerve with cornered terrorists holding hostages. A commando-type assault is only launched when terrorists begin killing hostages. Hostage situations are not uncommon to police of most nations when criminals seize hostages to bargain for their freedom; women and children sometimes become hostages in domestic tragedies; and so a certain amount of experience and know-how has been gained; it is just a matter of refining it to adjust to a terrorist incident. The principle is that there should be no bargaining with terrorists, but it is one in which politics occasionally interfere.

Some nations have specialized military forces, capable of coping with either low-intensity operations, or terrorist incidents, but they are seldom used in Western countries. The Americans have the Green Berets (military commandos) and SEALS (naval commandos), which are part of the armed forces, and are mainly used overseas. The British have the Special Air Services Regiment (SAS), which was used at the siege of the Iranian Embassy in London during 1981, after which it was decided that the Metropolitan Police should have its own armed counter-terrorist team. The SAS is now mainly employed in NI on surveillance tasks, and abroad, as evidenced by the Gibraltar incident.

There are divided views as to whether airliners should carry armed guards, or 'Sky Marshals', as the Americans call them, on passenger air flights, to take action against would-be skyjackers should the occasion arise. The consensus of airline pilots' associations is against such a practice, and that in the event of a skyjack it is better to obey terrorists' instructions than risk an airborne gun-battle, when bullets may puncture the fabric and cause sudden disastrous decompression. However, a number of national airlines do carry armed guards notably El Al, Pakistan, Egypt, certain Arab ones, and probably those of South Africa, Aeroflot and the Eastern bloc countries. Their reasoning is that if it is known there are armed guards incognito among the passengers, it acts as a deterrent. Sky Marshals were unsuccessful in preventing the skyjack of the Egypt Air aircraft to Malta.

Internment without Trial When terrorist suspects are arrested in Western countries, if evidence against them is inconclusive, the best the authorities can do is to extend their time in detention for a few days, in order to allow the police to make further inquiries. Then, if further evidence is not forthcoming, the suspects have to be released. If terrorists are caught red-handed evidence is usually available in plenty, or if there is ample forensic or circumstantial evidence, the terrorist can be formally charged, and remanded in detention for trial.

When terrorists have plenty of local support, such as in parts of NI, Corsica or in Basque territory, they are often sheltered by a sympathetic community. In such scenarios it is almost impossible (supergrasses excepted perhaps) to persuade local individuals to give evidence in Court against compatriot local terrorists. Threats of death to the witness and his family, are not idle ones. This means that often there is no point in the police arresting 'known terrorist suspects', without ample evidence, only to have to release them again, and have the frustration of seeing them at liberty without being able to do anything about it.

One method of tackling this problem is 'internment without trial', which in Western countries requires special temporary legislation or government order. It is a difficult political decision which no Western government relishes, as it has the disadvantage of grinding against enunciated democratic civil rights and justice; allows terrorist groups to cast odium on the government; and evokes sympathy for the terrorists from abroad. Another disadvantage of herding numbers of suspected terrorists and their sympathizers together in prisons or detention camps is that it turns the prison into an indoctrination centre, where detained leaders, some even allowing themselves to be deliberately detained for the purpose, have their members captive, and are able to further indoctrinate and instruct the committed, work on the doubters and waverers, and punish the backsliders. One advantage, however, is that the incidence of terrorism tends to decline when many activists are in detention.

The old IRA was forged in internment camps in Wales, prior to which they were not taken seriously by either the British Government or the Roman Catholic people of Ireland. The British tried internment without trial in NI, but it proved to have more disadvantages than advantages, and was not worth the political bother. Totalitarian and Communist governments do not have this problem, as terrorists and their followers can be bundled in with political prisoners, with no questions allowed, and no information given.

The Media In Western countries with a free Press, the media has often been referred to as the 'Terrorists' Best Friend', because it usually freely and fully gives publicity which is their life-blood, often over-writing terrorist motives, exploits, successes and personalities, pandering to sensationalism, and over-emphasising trivia. But in some Western countries, such as Spain and Italy, the media is forbidden to publish any terrorist manifesto, communiqué or demand, or to praise terrorists or terrorism in any way. Police have difficulty in keeping essential information and operational plans confidential, as terrorists watching television, listening to the radio, or reading newspapers, are often told exactly what the security forces are doing, thus allowing terrorists and their accomplices time to make a run for it, or to go to ground.

The media are often urged to be more responsible in their coverage of terrorism, but in the competitive Western Press world, its exclusivity-seeking attitude means that self-censorship is seldom manifest. Police need the factor of surprise, even more than terrorists. One suggestion often put forward is that whenever a terrorist incident occurs, a terrorist is arrested, or a cache of arms is discovered, the matter should automatically become *sub judice* until a terrorist is charged with an offence (when it becomes *sub judice* anyway), or until the police feel that certain information can no longer be of any value or help to terrorism. Censorship in any form is repugnant to Western governments, and so the problem remains that the *sub judice* idea does not seem to appeal to many in authority. Totalitarian and Communist countries enforce censorship which handicaps terrorism, and one looks forward with interest to the evolution of the Soviet Glasnost on the media in the USSR, and news of Soviet terrorism, so far largely hidden from us.

International Co-operation

Extradition An international, or even national, terrorist does not recognize national boundaries, as national security forces have to do. Clearly, it would be ideal if all nations would define, and recognize terrorism, so that terrorists could be easily extradited to the country that wants to bring them to justice, but there has always been a massive stumbling-block. Extradition agreements are sparse, and studded with exceptions; no general accord exists; and proceedings are fraught with national prejudices, political expediency, and sometimes outright malicious perversity. Many nations have traditions of granting political asylum to exiles fleeing from 'repressive or hostile' governments; and all have objections to such a general rule. Extradition of terrorists still depends upon current attitudes and prejudices of governments, even between ostensibly friendly states. In the current decade Britain shelters Balkan political exiles; America, Cubans and Irish; Arab states, Palestinians; the ROI, IRA members; India, Tamils, and so on; among these refugees are more than a sprinkling of terrorists.

When modern international terrorism suddenly developed its trans-world extensions, attempts were made in the United Nations to obtain a universal agreement on arresting and extraditing terrorists from sanctuary countries, but they made little headway because of opposition from those with axes to grind, because of demanded exceptions, or through sheer indifference. The perennial 'Freedom Fighter' or 'Terrorist' issue always raised its head to prevent consensus. For expediency, a few bi-lateral agreements were made which fell far short of the ideal. One was between the USA and Cuba, at the time of their confrontation in the 1960s, for the return of skyjacked aircraft and seajacked craft to their country of origin. It did not include the forcible return of fleeing political exiles (terrorists to one side or the other), but it was a small step in the right direction, and tended to ease tension.

Repression of Terrorism Convention Despairing of United Nations' action, the first major step was taken by the Council of Europe in 1977, when it produced the 'Repression of Terrorism Convention', which catered for either the extradition of terrorists from sanctuary countries, or for terrorists to be tried by the country in which they were arrested. This Convention was signed by seventeen (of the nineteen) member states, the exceptions being the ROI and Malta; but of the signatories, four still declared they would not extradite for political reasons, five others said they would not extradite their own nationals, and a few others insisted they would not extradite to a country that retained capital punishment. National governments are jealous of their sovereign power, and are reluctant to surrender any part of it, even for such a shining ideal. This Convention has only functioned partially, and selectively, and usually only when it suits a national interest, or the mood of the government. In this decade we have seen French governments ignoring extradition pleas from both Italian and Spanish governments; and Holland and Sweden rejecting British applications for the extradition of IRA terrorists.

Britain has long had an extradition problem with the ROI, where the RUC allege that at least 150 wanted IRA terrorists are living in comfortable freedom; all requests for their extradition being ignored or refused. Eventually in 1976, two analogous Acts were passed, one British and the other Irish, the object being to ease extradition proceedings, and which allowed for a terrorist to be brought to trial in either country. Despite these Acts, and up-dating legislation in attempts to plug legal loopholes, extradition proceeding for individuals in the ROI have seldom worked smoothly.

The ROI legal authorites often rejected British requests on technical grounds, such as warrants being incomplete. The Anglo-Irish Agreement of 1985, was designed to improve relations between the Dublin and Westminster governments, but the goodwill of the Irish Government and its judicial officers seems to be wanting in this respect. Irish commitment to the fight against terrorism is only partial. PIRA communiqués, statements and claims of terrorist exploits, are still issued through the Provisional Sinn Fein Office in Dublin.

Close technical liaison between senior career officers of national security forces is not only desirable, but necessary, in the fight against terrorism, so that intelligence can be exchanged, and to ensure that terrorists find no hiding-place, but this has always been retarded in Western nations by political leaders reluctant to allow government servants to deal directly with other national government servants; perhaps because they are reluctant to delegate any authority to a non-political official, and perhaps in case they conspire together in covert operations to catch terrorists, or in some way compromise the prejudices of their masters. Nevertheless, a degree of co-operation and trust at technical level has developed between national security forces, as instanced by the Gibraltar Three, and the arrest in Belgium of the Finance Director of the PIRA.

The so-called Trevi Group, once the Group of Seven, but now consisting of the interior Ministers of the twelve EEC member states, meets periodically to coordinate security and intelligence matters. The Trevi Group, has recently discussed subjects that include sequestering funds held in banks by terrorist groups; pursuit of terrorists across national borders; exchange of forensic evidence; and a common policy for asylum seekers. It has issued a Report (*The Common Fight against Terrorism*), listing a few proposals, but is having difficulty in finding common agreement on them, as so many members demand exceptions. The Trevi Group is a convenience forum, without teeth; and unity of action against terrorism, even between like-minded nations, still has a long way to go.

State Terrorism Certain States, including Algeria, Libya, Syria and South Yemen, and perhaps others such as Egypt, Greece and Italy, continue to dabble in International State Terrorism. The question arises, how should they be dealt with by other nations, discouraged, or penalized? So far the stiffest reprobation is for a complainant state to sever diplomatic relations with the offending one; such as Britain did with Syria; but after a while, as tension eases diplomatic contacts are gradually restored with nothing seeming to change.

The usual suggestion that arises after some exploit that involves International State Terrorism, is that the offending country should be completely ostracized by all nations, and all diplomatic, trading, financial and communication, including transport by air, sea or land links with it be severed. This often-repeated suggestion never gets much support as so many diverse vested interests are involved, and the familiar barrier of 'One State's freedom fighter is another State's terrorist' obtrudes, and the idea is pushed aside. The only way nations seem to be able to co-operate with one another against terrorism, is when it is in their direct interest to do so, or if it will benefit them in some way. The London Accord has shown how cynically countries abandon common agreements when it suits their purpose.

The Fight Goes On Terrorism in its various forms remains endemic, and accordingly the fight against it can only be a containing one of 'win some, lose some', with both security forces and terrorists having their successes and failures. The 1980s saw immense improvements in Western security forces, several of which were reorganized, modernized and re-orientated, with some adopting new scientific attitudes towards intelligence gathering and international co-operation.

The 1980s is a decade of supergrasses and show trials; of hostage-taking and suicide-truck drivers; of spectacular terrorist success in skyjacking, and massive explosions that cost hundreds of lives; but scores of terrorists have been killed by the security forces, and hundreds, perhaps thousands, languish in prison, many of whom will remain there for many years yet; a heavy Middle East imprint has been made on International Terrorism; while nationalism has proved to be a more durable motivation than Marxism, or any other extreme ideology. Hampered by political interference, the fight against terrorism is likely to continue in much the same spasmodic manner into the next decade.

POSTSCRIPT

THE bloody saga of terrorism has continued on much the same pattern as before, with persistent daily rumbles of minor incidents plus the occasional spectacular event. One of the most recent of the latter was the crash of a Pan Am 747 airliner on the small Scottish town of Lockerbie (December 1988), killing all 259 people on board and eleven on the ground. The aircraft, with many Americans on board, had been flying from Frankfurt, via London to New York. The cause of the crash was found to have been a Semtex explosion – Czechoslovakia, which is the sole manufacturer of Semtex, still refuses to give it an identifiable 'finger-print'. Unusually, so far no terrorist group has claimed responsibility for this disaster, which boosted the total killed in terrorist-related aircraft incidents during 1988 which to 333 (*Flight International*). Elsewhere in Britain, Welsh extremists have been burning English 'holiday homes', and Animal Rights activists have been setting fire to stores and shops that sell products of animal skins. Meanwhile the police have thwarted planned IRA bombing campaigns in England, by discovering secret caches of arms and explosives. The British Government banned press interviews with terrorists.

In NI the toll from IRA attacks on the security forces, which were extended to British soldiers on the Continent, continued to mount. In both NI and the ROI several terrorist caches of arms were unearthed, some with Libyan markings on them. Some seemingly perverse decisions were made over extradition proceedings, which did not improve British-Irish government relations. A senior IRA leader, Father Patrick Ryan, was arrested in Belgium, but a British request for his extradition was refused, and instead Ryan was sent back to the ROI, which also refused to extradite him to Britain. It is probable that Ryan may be tried in Dublin for terrorist offences, and there is talk of witnesses being able to give evidence by video-satellite without actually having to travel to the ROI, where some may have security problems. This procedure should become standard practice between countries, where witnesses are in one state and the trial in another, as it would do much to encourage them to come forward and avoid intimidation threats.

Trials of Action Directe leaders dragged on in France, evidence indicating that this organization was really the mainspring of Euro-Terrorism. It is suspected that AD members still at large, together with others, are lying low and planning a revival of Euro-Terrorism in 1992, when there will be freedom of movement within the EEC. In Spain, Emiliano Revilla, the industrialist kidnapped by ETA, was released unharmed (October 1988) after 259 days in captivity, a ransom reputedly in excess of $5-million having been quietly paid. The Spanish Government has refused offers from ETA for a cease-fire, as they were linked with the demand that negotiations would be held in public. France handed over more ETA members arrested in its Basque territory, probably preventing a resurgence of that group's activities in

Spain, a country uneasy and uncertain about what to do about revelations that GAL has been operating death squads. In West Germany, the trial of Hamadei, who admitted being involved in the TWA hijack of 1985, also dragged on.

The Hezbollah umbrella terrorist organization, based in Lebanon, is currently fighting desperately for its existence against the Amal group. The ending of the Gulf War (July 1988) tended to weaken its links with Tehran, but it still holds several European hostages, although others have been released, reputedly for large ransoms and political favours. Yasir Arafat, leader of the PLO, renounced terrorism (January 1989), but he has little control over some of the maverick extremist factions in his umbrella organization; while the elusive Abu Nidal still roams actively through the Middle East and adjacent regions, leaving footprints of blood behind him. Armenian terrorists have not been active of late, so perhaps the death of Hagop Hagopian was really their death knell.

19 January 1989

Index